Henry Hallam

Twayne's English Authors Series

Sarah Smith, Editor
Tufts University

TEAS 330

HENRY HALLAM
Portrait by G. S. Newton
Courtesy of the National
Portrait Gallery, London

Henry Hallam

By Peter Clark

Bromham, Bedfordshire, England

Twayne Publishers • Boston

Henry Hallam

Peter Clark

Copyright © 1982 by G.K. Hall & Company
All Rights Reserved
Published by Twayne Publishers
A Division of G. K. Hall & Company
70 Lincoln Street
Boston, Massachusetts 02111

Book production by Marne B. Sultz

Book design by Barbara Anderson

Printed on permanent/durable acid-free
paper and bound in the United States of
America.

**Library of Congress Cataloging in
Publication Data**

Clark, Peter.
Henry Hallam.

(Twayne's English authors series : TEAS
330)
Bibliography: p. 136
Includes index.
1. Hallam, Henry, 1777–1859
—Criticism and interpretation.
I. Title. II. Series.
PR4735.H4Z63   907'.2024 [B]   82-2974

ISBN 0-8057-6818-1   AACR2

To my
Mother
and the memory of
my Father

Contents

About the Author
Preface
Acknowledgments
Chronology

Chapter One
Life and Times   1

Chapter Two
The Middle Ages   30

Chapter Three
Constitutional History   61

Chapter Four
Literary History   89

Chapter Five
Hallam's Place in Historical Literature   108

Notes and References   119
Selected Bibliography   136
Index   141

About the Author

Peter Clark was born in 1939 in Sheffield, England, and graduated in 1962 with a degree in history and political institutions from the University of Keele. From 1962 to 1963 he taught mathematics at Ankara College, Turkey, and English at the British Council, Ankara. In 1963–64 he was a research student at Downing College in the University of Cambridge and for two years from 1964 was tutorial assistant in history at the University of Leicester. For a year he taught at a College of Art in Scotland, and in 1967 he joined the staff of the British Council, since when he has worked in Spain, Jordan, Lebanon, and the Sudan.

During the 1960s he was researching on the life and work of Henry Hallam. He was awarded the degree of Ph.D. by the University of Leicester in 1970 for a thesis on the subject.

From 1970 to 1971 he studied Arabic at the Middle East Centre for Arab Studies, Lebanon. He is the author of *Three Sudanese Battles* (1977) and has translated, from Arabic, Ismat Hasan Zulfo's *Karari: The Sudanese Account of the Battle of Omdurman* (1980). As well as two articles on Hallam, he has published articles and reviews on the Middle East in the *Times,* the *Guardian, Middle East International,* the *Times Literary Supplement, Middle East Education,* and the *Army Quarterly.*

Peter Clark has given lectures on English literature and on Arab history at universities in England, Lebanon, Jordan, and the Sudan. At present he is the representative of the British Council in the Yemen Arab Republic.

Preface

The study of past historical literature has many uses. In the first place, it is possible to study the stages in the evolution of the present-day historical perspective. Second, a study can be made of how one man's thought and intelligence, limited inevitably by circumstance, upbringing, and environment, deal with issues of historical controversy. Third, a study of a historian or historians of one generation leads to an understanding of that generation's historical perspective. Fourth, the study of past historical literature sharpens an historical awareness and critical faculty in the practice or the study of history today.

The life and work of Henry Hallam is worth examining for all these reasons. Hallam worked and wrote at the same time as Scott, Carlyle, Macaulay, and Ranke. In his day he was regarded as the doyen of English historians, and no gentleman's library was complete without a set of Hallam. He was working when historical fashions were changing, and the decline in his reputation coincided with the development of more scientific methods. Yet the framework he used and the conclusions he reached were substantially those of his successors. The archive work of Stubbs, Froude, and Gardiner tended to corroborate Hallam not because Hallam was "right" but because the Victorian historians were working with the same terms of reference. Hallam saw himself as a philosophical historian—in the tradition of Hume, Robertson, and Gibbon. Thus Hallam is an essential link between Hume and Stubbs.

Hallam's life was comfortable. He was born in the same decade as Scott, Wordsworth, Coleridge, Southey, and Jane Austen. The French Revolution was a challenge to him as to most of his generation. Industrialism, a changing society, an expanding world had to be assimilated into one's view of life and one's temporal position in the world. Hallam faced these challenges in a conservative but open-minded way.

Hallam's work went through many editions in his own lifetime but his popularity tailed off after 1870. It can be inferred that his work had an appeal to the generation 1830–1870, and helped in the making of the historical consciousness of that generation. Hallam's works were essential reading for many people. The queen, Gladstone, and Disraeli all read them. John Bright read Hallam aloud to his wife[1] and F. D. Maurice commended the *Constitutional History* to working men in 1866.[2] His work appeared even in fiction. Alton Locke read the *Middle Ages* and the *Constitutional History* in prison, made "copious notes and extracts" but—alas—"found them barren to my soul."[3]

The mental framework of Hallam is no longer that of our own day, yet a reading of Hallam throws some light on to the problems he dealt with. As with the work of David Hume, one is conscious of being with an acute mind that is exercising itself on problems of the past.

Henry Hallam has been the subject of no biography. His surviving daughter asked Sarah Austin to write a memoir. She refused, saying "wait for M. Mignet."[4] Mignet, the French historian, wrote a eulogy which is laudatory but neither very informative nor particularly perceptive.[5] Hitherto the fullest account of his life has been in Leslie Stephen's short article in the *Dictionary of National Biography*. The first chapter of this study is intended to record some of the activities of Hallam's life, his development and personal circumstances, particularly as they relate to his own historical work.

The three following chapters deal with his three major works. An attempt is made to place the writings in context. This involves a discussion of many topics related to his historical writings: medievalism, the legal and historical approaches to the English constitution, Whig history, historical methods, standards of criticism, concepts of the Renaissance. Insufficient attention has hitherto been paid to Hallam's work in relation to these topics.

The last chapter attempts to put Hallam's work in the environment of the practice of history at his time. Hallam is seen as one of the last of the philosophical historians who continued some of the controversies that raged in the seventeenth century and who was overtaken by changing fashions and styles in historical literature.

All references to Hallam's works are to the first editions, unless otherwise stated.

Peter Clark

Bromham, Bedfordshire, England

Acknowledgments

This study is based on a thesis submitted for the degree of doctor of philosophy at the University of Leicester in 1970. I am grateful to the two supervisors I had, Mr. Duncan Forbes of Clare College, Cambridge, and Professor Jack Simmons of the University of Leicester, for their guidance, and to my external examiner, Professor G. F. A. Best of the University of Edinburgh, for his helpful comments.

Sir Arthur and Lady Elton gave much encouragement in the early stages of my work. I also benefited from several discussions with the late T. H. Vail Motter. The late Sir John Murray kindly gave me permission to consult some letters of Hallam in the archives of the publishing house of John Murray.

I would like to thank the librarians of many libraries who gave me assistance, in particular Mr. H. F. R. Wing of Christ Church Library, Oxford; Mr. A. Halcrow of Trinity College Library, Cambridge; and the librarians of the Massachusetts Historical Society, Boston, the University of Cambridge, the University of Leicester, and the University of St. Andrews. Dr. Aubrey Newman of the University of Leicester was kind enough to give me access to his microfilms of the Stanhope papers.

Chronology

1777	9 July, birth of Henry Hallam at Windsor, Berkshire.
1790–1795	Eton College.
1795–1798	Christ Church, Oxford.
1799–1806	Barrister on the Oxford circuit.
1804–1809	Writer for *Edinburgh Review.*
1806–1825	Commissioner of stamps, a government sinecure.
1807	January, marries Julia Elton of Clevedon Court, Somerset.
1811	2 February, birth of son, Arthur.
1818	*Middle Ages.*
1827	*Constitutional History.*
1828	Reviews by Macaulay and Southey of *Constitutional History.*
1828–1831	On Council of London University.
1833	15 September, Arthur Hallam dies in Vienna.
1834–1840	Treasurer of Statistical Society.
1837	*Literature of Europe,* volume 1.
1839	*Literature of Europe,* volumes 2–4.
1845–1849	President of the Royal Society of Literature.
1846	Rejects offer of baronetcy made by Sir Robert Peel.
1848	*Supplemental Notes.*
1850	Son, Henry Fitzmaurice Hallam, aged twenty-six, dies at Siena, Italy.
1852	*Literary Essays and Characters.*
1859	21 January, Henry Hallam dies at Bromley, Kent.

Chapter One

Life and Times

Background and Childhood

The Hallams came from professional Lincolnshire stock. The grandfather of the historian, John Hallam (1693–1762), was a surgeon in Boston and was twice mayor of that town. His brother, Isaac, was an apothecary and a minor Lincolnshire poet, and the family, until the mid-eighteenth century, were generally well-rooted to their locality. John Hallam's only surviving son, also called John, received his early education from Boston Grammar School but, presumably after the influx of some money into the family, moved to Eton College in 1743 and on to King's College, Cambridge.[1] As a young man he was the tutor to the third duke of Buccleuch from whom he received an annuity of £300 a year.[2] This helped toward a respectable career in the Church of England. He became a canon of Windsor and was for many years dean of Bristol. He married Eleanor Roberts, daughter of the provost of Eton, and was the father of Henry Hallam, the historian. The dean died in 1811 and was buried in St. George's Chapel, Windsor. The family by this time had achieved financial independence: estates in the villages round Boston, and—the fruits of a legacy from a distant cousin—more property around Birmingham and West Bromwich.[3]

Henry Hallam was born at Windsor on 9 July 1777. From an early age he showed an aptitude for literature and learning. Several poems of his childhood survive, displaying imagination and ingenuity but also a pessimism that was to be a characteristic of him all his life. One of his poems is called "Ode to Melancholy," and in "To Hope," written in December 1788, he wrote "And hope is gone, and naught is left for me / But fell despair and misery profound."[4]

In 1790 or 1791 Hallam attended Eton College. He spent four or five years there. He seems to have been a studious youth, sufficiently studious to acquire the nickname "Doctor" from his contemporaries.[5]

Student Days

After Eton Hallam went up to Christ Church, Oxford, in 1795. Christ Church at this time was under the deanship of Dr. Cyril Jackson. Dean Jackson's quarter century of office was a turning point in the history of the college. Before his time Christ Church had been the resort of aristocrats chiefly interested in the three H's—horses, hounds, and whores. He transformed the college into a house of intellectual eminence and Tory politics—the nursery of Canning, Peel, and the young Gladstone.

At Christ Church Hallam was one of a hundred and twenty undergraduates.[6] Among them he made several close friends with whom he corresponded for the rest of *their* lives—for Hallam survived nearly all his early friends and contemporaries. Among them was Peter Elmsley, prodigiously fat, a classical scholar who has been compared to Porson. Elmsley was later to take orders, and become an Edinburgh reviewer and the Camden Professor of Ecclesiastical History in the university.[7] Another was Harry Wintour, a hypochondriac who married and died before he was thirty, leaving two or three very young children. A third, and, for Hallam, the most important, was Lord Webb Seymour. Hallam tended to be reserved toward his friends and his family, but to Lord Webb he was able to speak and write with candor and confidence. Seymour was a couple of years older than Hallam, a son and brother of successive dukes of Somerset. He had a wide range of intellectual interests and took life extremely seriously. "None of his peculiarities," recalled an Edinburgh friend, Henry Cockburn, "amused his friends more, or was a more frequent subject of joking to himself than the slowness and vastness of his preparations."[8] Seymour's main field of interest was geology and, after leaving Oxford, he made his home in Scotland in order to study further and to be near the Scottish geologist, John Playfair.[9]

Most undergraduates of the day were given a grounding in the classics and mathematics. In the next few years at Christ Church, tutors were supervising the reading of such works as De Lolme's *Constitution of England* and Robertson's *Charles the Fifth*. However, Hallam's supervised work was, for the most part, conventional—a solid diet of classics and mathematics.

From a commonplace book of this time that survives[10] we learn that in the autumn of 1796 when he entered his second year at Christ Church he started to learn German from a German teacher three times a week. He read thoroughly, in addition to his set work, Paley's books and Henry's *History of England*.

In 1797 Hallam's scheme of work intensified. He was learning Italian and reading Tasso. He read English poetry from Milton to Southey, books on chemistry and philosophy, Adam Smith and Edward Gibbon. In September, reviewing his intellectual progress of the past year, he found

upon the whole not much cause for dissatisfaction. I have obtained in the first place some knowledge of Roman History, by reading Livy, Polybius, some lives of Plutarch and some parts of Appian. To this I have added some ideas of the Roman constitution: but in this I feel myself still very deficient. . . . While I contemplate with some though not unmixed pleasure, what I have done, I must not overlook what I have omitted. In the course of this year, nothing has been done in Mathematics, & very little in Modern History: Poetry has been unaccountably neglected, & with it all attention to style. I have written literally nothing which I think never happened in any former year.

Hallam started his third year at Oxford badly. "These three weeks have flown away like a dream, & I look back with shame on my intellectual idleness." However, this indolence was soon remedied. We soon find him reading Belsham, Burnet, Hume, Dio Cassius, Blackstone, Vergil, Euclid, Aristotle, Rapin. But, like Dr. Johnson, Hallam was overwhelmed by an unjustified sense of his own idleness. "Another year has now elapsed," he wrote in September 1798,

since I last reviewed the progress of my knowledge. Conscious of many interruptions from necessity, & of far more from indolence, I almost tremble to look back upon this period. At the conclusion of the last year I find resolutions to prosecute the study of the Roman History of Anatomy, Chemistry & German & to pay attention to style. I find also a determination to pursue political research. Of all this how little has been done? In the first certainly not much, in the others nothing.

Some of this reading, in particular the mathematics, was prescribed and supervised by his Oxford tutor, but a pattern is emerging. A letter from Seymour in 1802[11] suggests that Hallam at one time considered a career in politics. Most of his friends and the home influence tended to be Tory, but there are, at this stage, no clear indications of his political views nor of his reaction to such writers as Hume and Burnet. Belsham he thought was "Whig almost unto democracy," a remark more likely to be uttered by one who disagreed with a vigorous Whig line than otherwise. It is possible that uncertain views, lack of patronage, and a more studious temper led him to choose the profession of law. This possibilty is strengthened by the evidence of a switch in his reading during his last year at Oxford to Blackstone and to a study of modern English history.

Young Lawyer

Trinity term 1798 was the last that Hallam kept at Christ Church. He took his degree early in the following year and, after a few months at his father's house at West Bromwich, took up his chambers in Lincoln's Inn, London, and pursued his studies in law. In his first postgraduate year the pace of reading fell off and the record stops with a final retrospect, full of self-reproach, in September 1799. "From the task of self-examination," he wrote then,

I am ever willing to escape, for the retrospect is seldom pleasing. What I might have done, had I early & unremittingly devoted my attention & exertions to the improvement of such faculties as have been given to me, I know not; but too much, I fear, has been lost, both of time and power, to be ever retrieved. Another year has elapsed, since I last reviewed the state of my acquisitions, & if I had cause to regret when that last survey took place that necessity had deprived me of much & that indolence had been more injurious, the present account is still less in my favour. . . . May the ensuing year be more propitious.[12]

For the next three years—until 1802—Hallam spent most of the year in London. For two or three months in the summer he stayed with his parents at Windsor or at West Bromwich. The latter town was at this time an industrial village in a rapidly developing area of light industry, and in successive summers he entertained Oxford friends there. In

August 1799 he took a friend to "Mr. Boulton's. He showed us some parts of the Mint and permitted us to see the Manufactory." They also examined the manufacture of buttons, buckles, whips, papier mâché, and swords. "This is truly wonderful & perhaps raises our ideas of the division of labour beyond any thing. . . . On the whole, nothing can be more wonderful than the manufactures of this great trading town [Birmingham]: the mind, especially of one unskilled in the arts & sciences connected with them, is incompetent to apprehend every thing, or to retain more than a very small part of what it apprehends."[13]

In May 1802 Hallam wrote to Seymour reflecting on the four years since he had left Oxford. "When I compare my general literary assiduity during the last three years, with my Oxonian life, I have no reason to regret a diminished velocity in the intellectual progression. I have, I hope, though not by dint of philosophical investigations, yet by the natural effect of time on the faculties, acquired stronger habits of judging, and better habits of reflecting than I possessed at Oxford."[14] Six weeks after writing this, Hallam made his first trip abroad. He crossed to Dieppe and visited Paris.[15] But we know nothing more of this first continental excursion.

Hallam's career as a barrister lasted until 1806. He practiced on the Oxford circuit. Little is known of his legal career beyond the fact that he dealt with minor cases concerning, among other things, election petitions, unpaid rents, and other property disputes.[16]

Edinburgh Reviewer

In 1804 Hallam started an association with the *Edinburgh Review* that was to last for five years. He met one of the original reviewers, Francis Horner, on the latter's visit to London in March 1803,[17] but the connection was probably strengthened by Elmsley, who was an early contributor, and Seymour, who was at this time an Edinburgh resident and helped to plan the first issue of the *Review* in October 1802.[18] From a letter from the editor, Francis Jeffrey, to "Hallam, Esq," written in December 1804, it seems that Elmsley had asked Jeffrey to let Hallam review Plowden's *Irish History*. This was not possible, but Jeffrey wrote—"I am anxious to dip you in our ink with as little delay as possible." Horner had told Jeffrey that Hallam's "Historical information is accurate and extensive" and Hallam was offered several books to review.[19] There was indeed little delay, and Hallam's first contribution was a review of the *History of France from the Time of its Conquest by Clovis in A.D. 480* by Alexander Ranken.[20]

The following year Hallam wrote two important articles. The first was a review of Payne Knight's *Inquiry into the Principles of Taste.* In this Hallam took Knight to task for an incorrect rendering in Greek of a passage from Gray, although it was "very presumptuous of us Scotchmen to contend about Greek at all." Unfortunately the Greek translation was actually some lines of Pindar which Hallam failed to recognize. This blunder aroused some scorn and led Byron to sneer at "classic Hallam much renowned for Greek" in *English Bards and Scotch Reviewers.* This blunder was probably also the origin of Hallam's reputation in the next decade or so of being a pedant with a higher regard for precision than for accuracy. It was possibly another Edinburgh reviewer, Sydney Smith, who never saw eye to eye with Hallam, who coined the unkind nickname of "Bore Contradictor."[21]

Jeffrey, however, was generally pleased with the review. "What do they say," he asked Hallam in February 1806, "to your Knight in London? I have heard that your critique on the Greek verses is objectionable . . . but you must fight your own battles if it comes to fighting—for I am but a poor hand at quarters—if there is to be no fighting I have no objection to lie down and be licked for you." In the same letter Jeffrey asked Hallam to undertake a review of a pamphlet on the Catholic question. "The catholic question is difficult ground," he wrote, "but I confide in your discretion and must freely commit it to you. You may depend on the [ut]most secrecy for as long a period as you think proper. I have that qualification for the keeper of a den of conspirators." The article was, however, delayed. Hallam was, at this time, as we shall see, taking up his new job as commissioner of stamps. The delay brought down the wrath of the harassed editor, who wrote in May, "I reckoned securely upon your review of the catholic question & the other articles you spoke of for last no. & really thought myself entitled to some notice of the disappointment that was awaiting me—but you failed—& Horner & Herbert & Elmsley all followed your example & left me without the slightest warning to encounter the evil day of publication."[22] Jeffrey's industry, versatility, and resource did not fail him, however, and of the seven articles whose authorship is known, no fewer than six were written by the editor himself.[23] Hallam's article duly appeared in the next number, and in it he added his voice to those of Sydney Smith and other reviewers in calling for an end to the political restrictions on Roman Catholics. "We may venture to lay it down as a general proposition," Hallam wrote, "that all restrictive laws which exclude certain classes of men from political stations are, in their immediate operation, oppressive and impolitic."

This article pleased Jeffrey. He wrote to Hallam: "The excellence of your last article on the Catholic question—both as to reasoning information and temperament lead me to prefer some article upon the interesting and ticklish topics of our immediate & domestic policy."[24] However Hallam did not write on political questions of the day, although a review of a translation of Filangieri's *Principles of Legislation* in 1807 was probably his. In this, the statement of political views was consistent with Hallam's outlook all his life. In the article he considered that the names of Tory and Whig are "sometimes, idly enough, kept up." But the ideas to which it may be permissible to give the name "Whig" are there: a belief that the source of authority was the people and a defense of the liberty of the press.

A further article in 1808 reveals Hallam's political views. In a review of Coxe's *Memoirs of the House of Austria* in April 1808 Hallam scorned the overrated role of kings. "No man has a right to fill three quarto volumes with the history of the House of Austria, or of any other house whatsoever. It is not with families, but with subjects, that the dignity of history converses. Separately considered, the house of Austria has no more claim to our attention, than any other private family in Europe." But this hostility to monarchism did not prevent him from disapproving from some of the *Edinburgh Review* articles, which, in 1807 and 1808, were moving in a leftward direction,[25] and Jeffrey was writing in June 1808: "I thank you for your monitions about party violence—but it is difficult to repress the excesses of indispensable contributors." This was a singular defense. One of the principal writers of "violent" articles was Jeffrey himself. But an editor would naturally think himself indispensable. A few months later, Jeffrey was obliged to be on the defensive again. "I am increasingly obliged to you," Hallam was told, "for your candour and good counsel—I am as much vexed as anyone could be at our step but I hope it will be our last."[26]

But it was not to be. In the twenty-fifth number, October 1808, Hallam reviewed Walter Scott's edition of Dryden. In the same number, however, was the article under the title of "Don Pedro

Cevallos on the French Usurpation of Spain." This was written, it is believed, jointly by Jeffrey and Brougham. It called for a reform of the British constitution, and, by way of praising the Spanish patriots who had revolted against Napoleon, gave implicit approval to the political activities of the masses. By association, the idea of democracy was countenanced without disfavor. This article provoked a storm of protest and abuse. It offended Grey and the Holland House Whigs. Walter Scott withdrew his support from the *Review,* and three months later the rival *Quarterly Review,* firmly Tory, but otherwise modeled on the *Edinburgh Review,* appeared under the auspices of Canning, Southey, and Scott himself.[27] Hallam, too, was shocked at the article and Jeffrey pleaded with him. "I am afraid you are one of the abhorrers of Cevallos—& may think it great assurance in me to approach you with the guilt of that seditious publication still unatoned on my conscience. . . . The clamour that has been raised against us & the rivalry which I fear is preparing makes it necessary not only that we should be cautious but strong in the next No. . . . May I not rely on your assistance in such a crisis?"[28] Hallam wrote two more articles in these early years—the first a review of Joinville and the second a favorable account of a translation of Hesiod by his own brother-in-law, Charles Abraham Elton. However, his connection with the *Review* lapsed in October 1809, possibly in consequence of the strongly democratic tone of articles in both the July and October numbers.[29] Jeffrey was distressed and hoped that Hallam would remain an adviser to the reviewers "either by telling me where I go wrong or by suggesting what you think should be attempted," and promised to be less political in future issues.[30]

The correspondence of Jeffrey to Hallam bears witness to Jeffrey's reputation as an editor. He treated the review in a proprietary manner; he was prepared to chop and change the articles submitted; and in dealing with a wide range of people his diplomacy was stretched to, and possibly beyond, the limits of honesty.

Domestic Changes

Three years before Hallam's break with the *Edinburgh Review* he changed his job and married. Although Hallam regarded legal training as most desirable for his sons, there is evidence that the day-to-day business of the law courts bored him.[31] Indeed, to judge from remarks in the *Middle Ages,* he found the practice and study of law incompatible with philosophical aspiration. The accumulation of "statute upon statute, and precedent upon precedent, till no industry can acquire, nor any intellect digest the mass of learning that grows upon the panting student"[32]—this accumulation made Hallam an advocate of law reform. "It would be a disgrace," he wrote, "to the 19th century if England could not find her Tribonian." He was released from these chores by his appointment to the office of commissioner of stamps—a post that required frequent attendance at the Stamp Office in Somerset House but was not otherwise exacting. He was able to take at least two months' holiday each year.[33]

The other event of 1806 was his engagement. At Eton Hallam had known Charles Abraham Elton, son of the Reverend Sir Abraham Elton, a cantankerous clerical baronet. Sir Abraham spent his long life at Clevedon Court, the family seat in Somerset.[34] Charles Abraham Elton had a sister, Julia Maria Frances, to whom Hallam became engaged in the autumn of 1806. They married in January 1807 at Clevedon. Hallam probably had the Eltons' house in mind when he wrote about the houses of the fifteenth-century gentry ten years later. "The unusual arrangement consisted of an entrance-passage running through the house with a hall on one side, a parlour beyond, and one or two chambers above, and, on the opposite side, a kitchen, pantry and other offices."[35] After their marriage the Hallams took a London house in Bedford Place. Henry Hallam was immensely devoted to his wife for the thirty-three years of their marriage. There were many children, only four of whom, however, reached adulthood and only one survived Hallam.

In the early years of his marriage, Hallam only occasionally stayed at West Bromwich. The estate was partly settled on Hallam and his wife and, after his father's death in 1811, he inherited the rest of it together with the property Dean Hallam possessed in the villages around Boston. The income from the rents of both properties varied. During the war he was receiving about £1,500 per annum from his Lincolnshire property and between £50 and £200 per annum from his Staffordshire estates. After 1815 this income remained steady but then rose to a peak in the mid-1820s: over £2,000 per annum from Boston alone.[36] From a surviving book of accounts we learn that his expenditure in 1812 was over £2,250. There is no record of his accounts in the twenties and thirties, but in 1848 when he was a widower with two dependent adult children, his annual expenditure was over £3,300.[37]

The Middle Ages

One of the consequences of Hallam's retirement from journalism was a greater leisure to write his first book. The form of *View of the State of Europe during the Middle Ages* took a long time to settle in his mind. Correspondence with Lord Webb Seymour between 1812 and 1817 reveals the state of his mind on this. Hallam in his letters discussed with great frankness his plans and ambitions as a writer. On the eve of publication even his own brother-in-law, Elton, was ignorant of the subject that Hallam had been working on for ten years.[38] But with Seymour every stage seems to have been discussed.

At first Hallam was not sure to what purpose he should put his talents. In 1812 he was still uncertain whether to write a book on the Middle Ages or on the English constitution. However, he considered that subjects of reasoning and taste were better suited to his talents and that these qualities had more scope in writing of "the manners, literature and statistical conditions of the middle ages."[39] Seymour aided him in his dilemma. "The English constitution," he wrote in April 1812,

you say, would occupy three years, but the larger work at least six.—And why should you be afraid to look forward six years?—Or even for a longer period?—Time is requisite for every great work, and the chances of life must be risked.—You observe that you have not resolved to dedicate your life to it!—To what nobler work, or, if executed with success, better calculated to secure a permanent reputation, could a large portion of your life be dedicated?—It appears to me also one for which your mind is peculiarly fitted. While I do not deny you considerable powers in speculation, I think that those powers are far more strongly manifested in judgment, than in innovation. You have read much, and though you have not read without reflection, yet your thoughts have always been much guided by books, and your views have rather leaned upon the opinions of others, as corrected by your own acute discrimination than upon any broad original basis, constructed from your own observation of nature and compilation of facts.[40]

Hallam found writing hard and progress slow. In a letter of 1813 he incidentally reveals the leisure of a civil service appointment in Regency times.

There are insuperable impediments in the way of making very rapid progress. The daily avocations of this office, destroying almost the whole of the morning, united to the increasing temptations of society, are very hostile to any steady and serious exertion. If I get a few days for reflection or writing undisturbed, or in the country, I easily perceive by the ground I gain, and by the pleasure of the journey, how much is lost by the ordinary habits of my life. Without mixing so much in society as other men, I find its dissipations increase on me, & with the distractions of private cares, & political castle building make my weeks slide away without moving one step forward in the prosecution of what is still my favourite plan.[41]

The work was published by John Murray in the spring of 1818 in two quarto volumes and sold at three guineas a set.

Abroad and At Home

Soon after the publication Hallam left England for four months. It was not curiosity alone that took him to Europe. During the winter he had been weakened by a "slow, remitting fever,"[42] and his route was partly determined by the wish to visit the Belgian health resort of Spa. He left England in late June with his "wife & child & 2 servants." They crossed to Calais and stayed in Antwerp to look at paintings by Van Dyck and Rubens; on to Brussels and the site of the Battle of Waterloo where the weather was bad "but not such as to prevent my forming a very good notion of that memorable field"; then to Spa where he stayed three weeks to take the waters. The family took the road up the Rhine valley recently constructed by Napoleon from Cologne. ("I shall praise nothing but its cathedral, a matchless specimen of Gothic architecture.") At Lucerne Hallam sent his wife on to Berne "where I rejoined her after a week of Alpine wanderings. Unfortunately almost the only rain that fell during my tour came on while I was on this excursion." They all went on to Geneva. Here Mrs. Hallam remained with the child, Arthur, who, though but seven years old, "became familiar with the French language which he had already learnt to read with facility." The father meanwhile went across to Chamonix where he was joined by

Peter Elmsley. Together they crossed into Italy by the Simplon Pass. Elmsley and Hallam spent four days in Venice and visited Milan and Turin before returning by Mont Cenis to Geneva. Hallam then accompanied his son and his wife, who was six or seven months pregnant, back to England, arriving home at the end of October. [43]

In his *Middle Ages,* Hallam had given a description of contemporary Tuscany: "Among uninhabited plains, the traveller is struck by the ruins of innumerable castles and villages, monuments of a time when pestilence was either unfelt, or had at least not forbad the residence of mankind."[44] In the first edition, the reader was referred to two travelers' works. In succeeding editions, there was no reference. He had seen for himself.

A domestic consequence to this tour was the premature birth of a daughter to Mrs. Hallam five weeks after their return. The daughter did not live and Mrs. Hallam was very ill. Hallam's growing family was dogged by fatality. Apart from Arthur, born in 1811, and Eleanor, born in 1817, at least two other children died in infancy before 1820. They included a son born in 1815 who was christened, in an uncharacteristic moment of patriotic enthusiasm on the part of his father, Charles William Waterloo Hallam.[45]

During these years Hallam lost two old friends. Francis Horner, who came to know Hallam through their association with the *Edinburgh Review,* was a Whig financial expert and a member of Parliament. He was, like Hallam at this time, a frequent visitor to Holland House and shared his interests in politics and European literature.[46] Horner died in Italy in 1817. Two years later Hallam suffered a greater loss with the death of Lord Webb Seymour in Scotland at the age of forty-two. Hallam read through his correspondence with Seymour and wrote a brief memoir. This was not published, however, until 1843. There were, between 1817 and 1843, several attempts to write a biography of Francis Horner and ultimately Horner's brother, Leonard, geologist and factory inspector, undertook the work. Hallam's memoir of Seymour appeared as an appendix.

Social Calls and His Second Work

During the early and mid-1820s, Hallam was busy on his second major work. He had, as we have seen, long contemplated writing a philosophical history of the English constitution and the work turned out, as he recognized, "in a great measure an extension of the eighth chapter of the 'View of the Middle Ages.'"[47] Nonetheless, he found time for his professional duties and for social and other activities. He continued to put in "almost the whole of the morning" at Somerset House as commissioner of stamps until 1825 when he retired with an annual pension of £500: a pension which he drew until 1850.[48] He became a regular visitor to Holland House where, in the words of W. S. Rose, Hallam's Etonian contemporary: "Often times hath the historic page / Been turned by honest Hallam, shrewd and sage."[49]

Hallam and Lord Holland were similar in temperament although Holland's son, Henry Fox, privately recorded his dislike of Hallam as "one of the most disagreeable members of society I ever have the misfortune to meet."[50] He was an acceptable visitor to Bowood, the Wiltshire seat of the marquess of Lansdowne, who, in 1824, became godfather to Hallam's son, Henry Fitzmaurice, and, in 1827, was the dedicatee of the *Constitutional History*. His extended circle of Whig and literary acquaintances included Sir James Mackintosh, who, by his brother-in-law, Sismondi, was a link with French literary society; Sydney Smith, who never seemed to overcome an early distaste for Hallam; and Thomas Moore, who frequently mentioned Hallam in his *Journal*. He also took an interest in learned societies. He became a Fellow of the Royal Society in 1821 and often took the chair at meetings of the Society of Antiquaries. Nor did work inhibit further expeditions with his family. In 1822 he took Arthur abroad for some months, visiting Geneva and joining Elmsley again in the Rhine Valley.[51] Three years later he went to Dublin by himself and was joined by Mrs. Hallam, Arthur, and his London doctor, Henry Holland, at Killarney after his sojourn there was prolonged by an accident which kept him bedridden for thirteen weeks.[52]

The Constitutional History of England from the Accession of Henry VII to the Death of George II was published by Murray in two quarto volumes in July 1827, and Hallam, as in 1818, immediately took his family abroad. After some time resident in Florence, the Hallams moved on to Rome, spending the winter there. From Rome he went further south to Naples and Amalfi. Observations at the latter city led to an added note in later editions of the *Middle Ages*.[53]

Arthur was now sixteen, an impulsive, sensitive youth. He caused some concern to his family by falling in love with Anna Wintour, daughter of Hallam's old Christ Church friend, Harry Wintour. As her father died in 1804, Anna must have been at least five or six years older than Arthur. This passion for Anna was shared by another visitor to Rome, James Milnes Gaskell, an Eton contemporary of Arthur, and each, with no feelings of jealousy, wrote to the other of Anna's qualities. Arthur poured out sonnets and love odes in English and Italian for her which embarrassed his father, who neither alluded to the incident nor published the verse when the *Remains* of Arthur were issued.[54]

The Row over the *Review*

It was also while Hallam was in Rome that he became involved in the biggest literary controversy of his life. His publisher, John Murray, was also the publisher of the Tory *Quarterly Review*—now edited by John Gibson Lockhart, son-in-law of Sir Walter Scott. In the January 1828 number the *Constitutional History* was reviewed by Robert Southey, apostate radical and fervent Tory. In an exceptionally long review, Southey undertook to destroy the ideas of philosophical history in general and Hallam's history in particular. To Southey, the work was misleading, absurd, and prejudiced. "The disagreeable temper of the book," Southey wrote,

would alone subtract much from the pleasure to be derived from the general ability which it displays, and the even tenour of its plain, strong, perspicuous style. Well, indeed, would it be were the spirit as English as the language: well, even if want of generosity, want of candour, and want of feeling were its worst faults. But in no English writer, who makes the slightest pretensions to morality and religion, have we seen the abominable doctrine so openly maintained, that the end justifies the means, and that conspiracy, treason, and rebellion, are to be treated as questions of expedience, laudable if they succeed, and only imprudent if they are undertaken without a sufficient likelihood of success.[55]

Before receiving a copy of the review, Hallam had heard that Southey was to write on his work and wrote rather nervously to Murray: "I value Mr. Southey's attacks not a farthing."[56] Nevertheless, when he did read the review, he was furious: furious at the tone of the article and furious at what he saw as a breach of etiquette on the part of John Murray, for having published such a hostile review of one of his own books. Hallam was so annoyed that he could not bring himself to write directly to

Murray, but used an intermediary, John Whishaw. Whishaw, a mutual friend of both Murray and Hallam, was an elderly solicitor and a frequent diner out at Whig houses, where he was known, on account of his discriminating taste, as the "Pope" of Holland House. In March Hallam read the article "with great contempt of it as an attack on myself, but with considerable uneasiness at its appearance in a publication of which he [Murray] is the proprietor. . . . [I]n some passages [it] exposes both the publisher and the author, as I conceive, to legal proceedings." He was grieved that "the number contained at least two extra sheets of Letter Press in order to make room for the unprecedented length of the article" and he looked on the matter "as being in the nature of a conspiracy, in which Mr Murray has been passively consenting, and his editor a leading party." Hallam threatened to withdraw his business connection from John Murray.[57] In April Whishaw wrote back with a message and defense from John Murray who had

received the rebuke with due submission, & acknowledged that you had great apparent reason to complain of *him* as well as of the author of the article. But he assured me as he has often done, that he is so completely in the hands of Southey and Lockhart as to be without even the power of remonstrance. This despotic system was fully established by Gifford: & it is now as fully maintained by the present Editor, whose connection with Walter Scott renders him very powerful. Southey, too, we all know, is a very impracticable man, especially on all subjects on which his Ecclesiastical & Political bigotry give him a particular interest.[58]

But Hallam was not satisfied with this. In reply he compared the relationship of Murray and Lockhart to "what sometimes happens in the management of private property, a weak man employs a very cunning one & ends by being in the power of his own agent."[59] Murray then wrote directly to Hallam, stating his idea of the role of the publisher and apologizing. The sale of the work had not, as Hallam feared, "been damped by any lukewarmness in its publisher, arising from any thing that might have been said against it, from his supposed deference to Tory opinions—if I were so foolish as to admit of much influence in the regulation of my business, its operation must, inevitably, be in the *selection* of what I should publish—& not in disposing of what had incurred both risque & expense in printing. No, I feel it a duty to publish with equal integrity—for Croker & Leigh Hunt—Scott

& Moore—Southey & Butler—Hobhouse & Gifford—Napier & Strangford." Murray considered the possible consequences of refusing to publish Southey's article. "What would have happened then?—the article would have appeared in a new Review with a statement appended which would have made it tenfold more efficient. . . . You cannot think me a fool enough, to allow a mere party feeling (if I had any) to risque the chance of selling what had cost me so much money—nor, I hope, base enough to sacrifice to it, such a valuable friendship as yours."[60]

Murray's apologia, combined with appeals for moderation from other friends and also, doubtless, the boost which the Southey article gave to the sales of the *Constitutional History,* all dissuaded Hallam from hasty action. Indeed, to judge from the tone of Hallam's letters to Murray after 1828, their relations were warmer than ever before.

While this was going on, Whishaw was scheming to get the book reviewed favorably in the *Edinburgh Review.* He considered Sir James Mackintosh as a possible reviewer, then the master of Dulwich College, Dr. Allen, and then William Empson of the East India College but "I have since heard . . . ," he wrote to Hallam in February, "that Jeffrey has engaged Macaulay to write the article—an arrangement which seems to be injudicious but which is probably too far gone to be altered."[61] Macaulay, at this time, was a young barrister and Fellow of Trinity College, Cambridge, aged twenty-seven. He was described around this time as "a youth of a Tory family, who was discovered to have a leaning towards the doctrine of the opposition."[62] Hence Whig suspicions. Whishaw, nevertheless, promised to do his best to "press" Macaulay.[63]

Macaulay's generous review[64] was, to a certain extent, a direct answer to Southey's attack. An allusive explanation of the attack is that Southey was by nature an extremist who failed to understand moderation. "In every furious partisan he sees either his present self or his former self, the pensioner that is, or the Jacobin that has been. But he is unable to comprehend a writer who, steadily attached to principles, is indifferent about names and badges, and who judges of character with equal severity, not altogether untinctured with cynicism, but free from the slightest touch of passion, party spirit or caprice." Elsewhere Southey appears as, and is condemned as, an admirer of Cranmer and of Strafford and as "an assailant of Mr. Hallam." In no place does Macaulay mention Southey or the *Quarterly Review* by name.[65]

Hallam and Social Reform

Henry Hallam returned to England in June 1828 and for the next few years became involved in a variety of public activities.

The first few decades of the nineteenth century saw revivals and foundations of universities in Europe and America. It became inevitable that there would be projects for a new university in England, and in 1826 the London University was established with strong backing from Scotch philosophers and Whig intellectuals. The first council of management included Henry Brougham, Lord Lansdowne, and John Whishaw. In 1827 they appointed a warden—a kind of secretary-registrar—Leonard Horner. [66] Hallam's relations with the University of Oxford seem to have been cool during the 1820s and 1830s [67] and he sent both his sons to Cambridge. This coolness, together with his connections with several of the founders, predisposed him toward London University, and Leonard Horner persuaded Hallam to join the council on his return from Italy, just as the first students were admitted. [68]

For the next three years the new institution underwent many difficulties which it often seemed unlikely to survive. Apart from difficulties of finance and status, a cumbersome constitution gave the professors no authority. The council of management and the professors became mutually antagonistic and the intermediary was Leonard Horner. Horner, however, was rather officious and personal rancor developed. In 1830 and 1831 Hallam was an active member of the council and was concerned in the crisis that led to the reorganization of the constitution, the retirement of Horner, and the subsequent revival of financial and public credit. This crisis was instigated by complaints about the professor of anatomy, G. S. Pattison, but the complaints developed into a personal squabble between Pattison and Horner. [69] Hallam steadily backed Horner, but in the spring of 1831 Horner announced his retirement. This was followed soon afterward by Hallam's own resignation. "I have given to its affairs," Hallam told Horner in July 1831, "a great deal of my time & attention [and] found the existence of obstacles which I had not adverted in the behaviour of many among the Professors. These & many other considerations determined me, as early as the commencement of the present session to withdraw from a situation of increasing & inevitable embarrassment, which encroached more on my time than was due to an institution as it seemed to me so little likely to be permanently or extensively beneficial."[70] In the autumn Hallam told Horner that "though not injured by it as you have been I heartily wish that I had never engaged in its affairs."[71]

Horner's successor was Thomas Coates. Coates was also secretary of the Society for the Diffusion of Useful Knowledge, another brainchild of the indefatigable Henry Brougham. Lord John Russell and the marquess of Lansdowne were also interested and active supporters of this essay in popular education.[72] Hallam became a member of the Committee of the Society, but he did not find his work "a very satisfactory office"[73] and in May 1836 resigned from the Committee because he was unable to attend as much as he ought and "for other reasons unnecessary to be mentioned."[74]

Work for the London University and for popular education was the closest Hallam got to the world of nineteenth-century reform. To the constitutional symbol of reform—the Reform Act of 1832—Hallam was implacably opposed. It was too revolutionary and democracy was unstable and dangerous. One of the implicit morals of his *Constitutional History* was that in the period after 1688 the English constitution attained the best possible human political arrangement. "Our practical constitution from 1688 to 1831," he wrote to Lord Mahon after 1832, "I hold to be among the best and happiest that has existed."[75] The Reform Act altered all this. "Il faudrait perfectionner, il ne faudrait pas transformer," he is reported to have told the duc de Broglie.[76]

The Death of Arthur

Arthur Hallam had gone to Trinity College, Cambridge, in October 1828. Here he was regarded as the outstanding member of a group of intellectuals. He developed his interests in literature and formed a close friendship with a morose and gawky youth from Lincolnshire named Alfred Tennyson. Arthur met Alfred's sister, Emily, and formed an even closer friendship with her. Henry Hallam was disturbed by his son's keenness to rush into both print and marriage. He succeeded in persuading the two young poets to postpone a proposed joint publication of verse. He failed to dissuade Arthur and Alfred from another joint venture, an expedition to Spain in 1830 to support the Spanish liberals. In the same year, the elder Hallam sought to quench Arthur's ardor for Emily. Although under twenty, Arthur wished to become engaged to Emily, but his father placed a veto on all correspondence and communication for one year. The veto was defied, and in 1832 Arthur was permitted to spend five weeks with the Tennysons in Lincolnshire, during which time he became engaged to Emily.[77] The following summer, Arthur accompanied his father on a European tour. They traveled as far as Budapest, and on 15 September 1833 in Vienna Henry Hallam returned from a constitutional to the hotel, Die Goldene Birne, and found his son in an armchair, dead. Arthur's wide circle of friends included many who later achieved distinction. There was an heroic quality about him, and his memory was revered by such acquaintances as W. E. Gladstone, W. M. Thackeray, and Richard Chenevix Trench.[78]

The body of Arthur followed the father back to England and was buried at Clevedon.

> The Danube to the Severn gave
> The darken'd heart that beat no more;
> They laid him by the pleasant shore,
> And in the hearing of the wave.[79]

Hallam assured Tennyson of his "heart-felt and lasting affection" for Emily[80] and to match words by deeds provided her with an annuity of £300.[81] This allowance did not cease when Emily married a midshipman, Jesse, a man of courage but of insufficient social position for some of Hallam's relations. This marriage shocked Hallam's Elton in-laws—"extraordinary—painful—unbelievable"—wrote Jane Elton of the marriage to her fiancé, W. H. Brookfield.[82]

Hallam himself wrote a memoir of his son. He wanted "to have the character of his mind, his favourite studies and pursuits, his habits & views, delineated. . . . I shall be very cautious as to printing anything that may too much reveal the secrets of his mind, either in prose or verse,—& this will preclude the possibility of printing some of his best compositions."[83] Thus in the privately printed memoir, written with the help of James Spedding and Alfred Tennyson, there were omitted references to that friendship with Anna Wintour, the expedition to Spain, the engagement to Emily, the differences of opinion with his father. The portrait that emerges is of a young intellectual Galahad of spotless purity and unfulfilled promise. Alfred Tennyson brooded over the loss of his friend all his life and his *In Memoriam,* published seventeen years after Arthur's death, struck a plangent note in mid-

Victorian religious feeling. The *Remains* of Arthur Hallam, privately printed in 1834, was published with his father's memoir unchanged in 1862.

Writings and Friendships

During the early and mid-1830s, apart from the hectic round of activities with learned societies, Hallam was busy writing. He wrote two more articles for the *Edinburgh Review*—one, a review of Lingard's work, prefaced by a survey of English historical writing; the other, a review of the work of Francis Palgrave. He was also busy writing the *Introduction to the Literature of Europe in the 15th, 16th and 17th Centuries.* Just as the *Constitutional History* grew out of the eighth chapter of the *Middle Ages,* so this third work was a development of the second part of the ninth chapter of his first work. Hallam thought highly of the originality and quality of his latest work which, he told his publisher, "I may say without great presumption, considering my age, literary experience and leisure as well as industry, there are not many persons in England so likely to execute as myself."[84] The first of four volumes was again published by John Murray at the price of fifteen shillings in September 1837 and the last three volumes in July 1839, also fifteen shillings each.

John Murray seems to have borne in mind Hallam's anger after the Southey review, for in the *Quarterly* there appeared a most favorable review, written, Hallam believed, by Henry Hart Milman, poet, churchman, and historian. But Hallam was hard to please. "I have not impudence enough," he wrote to Murray, "to read the article on my book in the Quarterly you have been good enough to send me without blushing, much less to think I deserve it. . . . The worst is that so high praise is apt to set the public against a book."[85] Macaulay, once again, wrote a warm review in the *Edinburgh Review.*

Association with Arthur Hallam's contemporaries had brought Hallam into contact and friendship with a younger generation during the 1830s and 1840s. He got to know the young William Gladstone who had been at Eton with Arthur. Hallam's family gave much assistance to Alfred Tennyson and his numerous brothers.[86] In the difficult years after 1834, when a hostile reception to a volume of verse had overawed the sensitive poet, Hallam was a constant source of encouragement. In 1845 he wrote to the prime minister, Sir Robert Peel, asking for a pension for Tennyson, "considered by many as the very first among the younger class of living poets."[87] Peel read some of Tennyson's poetry and told Hallam that he "formed a *very high Estimate* of his Powers."[88] However, Tennyson had to wait before he received an annual pension of £200.

A third close friend formed during the early 1840s was W. H. Brookfield, who had been at Trinity College with Arthur and who married a favorite niece of Hallam's, Jane Octavia Elton. In the late 1840s this marriage seemed to be on the rocks. Yet another of Arthur's Trinity contemporaries, William Makepeace Thackeray, was spending much time with Mrs. Brookfield. The family tried to paper over the cracks, but Hallam on at least one occasion felt obliged to remonstrate with Thackeray.[89]

Learning and Honors

The first four decades of the nineteenth century saw a development in the process of the rationalization of learning and the fragmentation of knowledge. Together with this process went a growing professionalism in some fields.[90] Hallam, as an educated man with polymathic interests, was active in the early days of a number of specialist societies that were to develop their own disciplines and techniques.

In the first half of the nineteenth century, statistics had more in common with political and social science than with mathematics. The shift to a mathematical emphasis in statistics was beginning in the 1830s. Charles Babbage, a distinguished Cambridge mathematician, was one of the driving forces in making statistics an independent discipline. He secured Hallam's interest in 1834. Hallam sought and secured the patronage of his friend, the marquess of Lansdowne,[91] and the Statistical Society was founded in 1834 with Henry Hallam as treasurer and Lord Lansdowne as president. He was treasurer for six years and, it is believed, drafted the first prospectus of the society. Hallam's interest was far from transitory. He took a keen interest in committees and contributed to the *Proceedings.* On his death, the Council of the Statistical Society referred to Hallam as "one of the most active supporters of this Society in its earlier days."[92]

Hallam was on the Council of the Geological Society, a vice-president of the Society of Antiquaries and of the Archaeological

Institute, and a trustee of the British Museum.[93] Some of these positions were purely honorary, but the busy journalist, William Jerdan, recalled the treat it was "to see the philosophical historian quite at home in all sorts of recreative excursions, or, especially, trudging in the train of geological explorations—with a satchel and hammer, and in a workmanlike costume, as if he had been a Sedgwick, Buckland or Murchison."[94]

During these years Hallam received a variety of honors from diverse associations. He was a member of the Athenaeum and of the exclusive bibliophile Roxburghe Club.[95] For four years, from 1845 to 1849, he was president of the Royal Society of Literature, and was made a bencher of the Inner Temple in 1841.[96] The University of Oxford was slow in giving him recognition. He did not take his master's degree until 1832,[97] but after the death of Thomas Arnold in 1842 there was some talk of his becoming Regius Professor of Modern History. Hallam professed unwillingness although in private he toyed with the idea. "I should like," he wrote to Lord Mahon, "to have given a series of lectures, & then resign the office."[98] Hallam's old college was very slow to acknowledge its distinguished alumnus. It was not until 1858, after the reforms of the 1850s, during the deanship of Henry Liddell and only a few months before Hallam's death, that he became an honorary Student of Christ Church. The United States was quicker in according him recognition. He was awarded the honorary degree of doctor of laws at Harvard University in 1848.[99] But Hallam's association with American intellectual life was unexpectedly cordial.

Additional duties of an honorific nature were pressed upon him in England. Peel appointed him a member of the Royal Commission—under the chairmanship of Prince Albert—set up in 1841 to consider fine arts in general and the interior decoration of the new Houses of Parliament in particular. Peel also, in his last months in office, offered Hallam a baronetcy. But "it would be challenging too unfavourable a comparison," Hallam wrote back, "if I, who have been little more than a collector of facts, should be placed on a level in reward with those who have carried forward the landmarks of human knowledge." He refused the honor because of "advancing years and the loss of those who would have shared it with me."[100]

Domestic and Social

During the 1840s Hallam was particularly devoted to the son, Henry. Round about 1840 his domestic circumstances altered much. In 1837 his daughter Eleanor (Ellen) suddenly died. Three years later he suffered the greater loss in the death of his wife at the age of fifty-seven. Hallam had the reputation of being a martinet to his family, and his relationship with his wife was hardly that of equal to equal, but there seems no doubt that he enjoyed an emotional stability derived from a secure marriage and a happy family life.

In spite of bereavements Hallam continued to lead a very active social life: he frequently entertained and was frequently a guest at dinner or breakfast with Macaulay or Mahon or Samuel Rogers or Monckton Milnes. It was at such entertainments that he increased his reputation as sage, critic, and talker rivaled only by Macaulay. "Never were such torrents of good talk as burst and spluttered over from Macaulay and Hallam," observed Lord Carlisle on one occasion.[101] A. F. Rio contrasted the styles of the two historians after a dinner at Rogers's in 1839.

It was who could say most in a given time—their volubility was frightful. Both had prodigious memories & a loose glibness equally prodigious. . . . Macaulay has the conceited trick of breaking off if only part of the audience are listening to him and he will walk to the other end of the room. He was too much for Hallam, apparently. His mind is quick, but has no tendency either to soar or to dive, its motions being only horizontal. He has sparkling eyes, and an opener face than Hallam's, which is an intellectual face too, with a sarcastic turn in the upper lip, but there's a hard muscle like a dyke across the middle of Hallam's face, which breaks a ripple from either direction, so that a smile from the eyes never reaches the lips, nor one from the lips the eyes.[102]

A regular guest at these dinners and breakfasts was Edward Everett, the American minister at the Court of St. James's. He felt drowned by the flood of oratory from the historians. "They talk so well and so instinctively," he recorded in his journal, "that I always listen to them with pleasure, but it is agreeable sometimes to be able to say a word. It is only by extreme vigilance in watching an opportunity . . . that you can ever say a word."[103] Before he became minister in 1841, when he was still only in his forties, Everett had had several distinguished careers as Unitarian minister, professor of Greek at Harvard, editor of the *North American Review,* United States senator, and governor of Massachusetts. He was gifted and personable and fitted into the social world with ease. During the early 1840s Hallam's acquaintance with Edward Everett ripened into friendship. Everett first met Hallam briefly in 1815 on his European tour with George Ticknor.[104] But the meeting was brief and in 1838 Guizot had to recommend Ticknor to Hallam again.[105]

But Hallam had got to know other American men of letters and of affairs. In the 1820s Hallam met Washington Irving,[106] who, with Hallam, had in 1830 received from the king a fifty-guinea medal awarded for historical eminence. Everett's friend, W. H. Prescott, in 1838 sent Hallam a copy of *Ferdinand and Isabella.*[107] The following year, another and closer friend of Everett, Daniel Webster, came to England and made a very great impression on Hallam.[108] But, if one may judge from the volume and cordiality of their letters, none of these other friendships were so warm and so firm as that of Hallam with Everett. Everett left London for good in 1845 and was replaced as minister twelve months later by George Bancroft. From Massachusetts, Everett pressed Hallam to make a summer ramble through the United States.[109] Hallam was tempted. "Believe me," he wrote back, "your country has a vast deal to attract & interest my curiosity both as to nature & man—& were I much younger & without ties at home, I might overcome my repugnance to two long voyages. . . . You have a tendency to what Carlisle [*sic*] calls hero-worship. . . . I have been much gratified by the testimonies of approbation that have reached me from the new world."[110] But Hallam's rambles were nearer at hand: Wiesbaden in 1841, Ryde in 1842, Dresden in 1843, Scotland in 1844, and Venice in 1845.[111]

Everett had strongly recommended his successor, George Bancroft, to Hallam, and the new minister called on Hallam three months before the latter's seventieth birthday. "Hallam has a countenance," he wrote glowingly to Prescott, "so full of benevolence, mildly radiant with a most gentle and kindly expression that he wins very rapidly on those that see him. The candor that pervades his nature and lights up his features makes you less regard a hesitancy of utterance. His good judgment shows itself as much in conversation as in his books: and his mind takes the widest range. He tells a pleasant story with animation and as for the extent of his learning, I do not pretend to fathom it."[112]

Last Publication and Literary Interests

In 1847 Hallam submitted to his publisher his last work, the *Supplemental Notes* to the *Middle Ages*. He had revised each edition of his work, but the growth of medieval studies and the publication of sources in the preceding generation had required a complete recasting of his earlier work. "The subject has been treated by so many since I began," he told Murray in 1845 when the publisher pressed for a new edition, "and so much light has been thrown on it by fresh publication of original matter that it would be a most arduous task to revise the whole work."[113] Even so he found the preparation of the *Notes* trying: "partly this is owing to the nature of the notes, all of which require care, being corrections or additions of more or less important matter—but partly also, I fear, to an increasing inaptitude for vigorous exertion of mind."[114] Hallam was at pains to avoid giving the impression that it was a new work,[115] but nevertheless he seemed uncertain about the role the book would take. He wrote to Mahon that "I did not expect that they [the *Notes*] would be much read, so connected are they with the main book, which ought to be in the hands of all who read them."[116] Yet he wrote to Lady Mahon that "it is chiefly designed for railway reading, but may save the trouble of looking into a dull volume of larger size."[117] In later editions of the *Middle Ages,* the *Supplemental Notes* were incorporated throughout the text. The work was well received in the summer of 1848 and Hallam was gratified.

The spring of 1849 saw the publication of the first two volumes of Macaulay's *History of England.* It made an immediate impact on both sides of the Atlantic, and Hallam's judgment was one of enthusiasm tempered with reserve. He wrote to Everett,

No book has ever had such success, as indicated by extensive sale—few have won more golden opinions. As usual I see a few symptoms of reaction; that is, more permit themselves to criticise than at first. The copiousness of knowledge, the readiness of the narration, the good sense of the method, judgments on many events, must strike everyone—perhaps we might wish a more sustained style, & the absence of some trivial expressions bordering on vulgarism: perhaps there is an excess of severity in appreciating characters & a little tendency to caricature on the *general* facts, though I believe him to be very accurate in circumstances.[118]

Harry

Hallam's surviving son, Harry, christened Henry Fitzmaurice, was now in his mid-twenties. As he grew to maturity, he seemed to his father and to friends of Arthur to be a providential compensation for the loss of the elder brother. When Harry was a fifteen-year-old boy at Eton, Hallam told Gladstone that "there are many points of resemblance in their characters"; six years later "the similitude in manners, character and even slight traits of language . . . is continually more and more striking."[119] Harry lacked the impulsiveness of his brother and never suffered Arthur's emotional upheavals; nonetheless, he gained the lasting affection of those who met him. After Eton, Hallam sent his son to Trinity College, Cambridge. After he graduated, Harry went in for a legal career although he had literary aspirations, possibly in the field of history.[120]

In July 1850, three weeks after the publication of *In Memoriam* had revived the memory of Arthur and had reminded the father of the resemblance of the two sons, Henry Hallam went off to the continent again. He lingered in the Rhine valley for a month and, the law term over, was joined by Harry. Father and son traveled on together through Bavaria and Austria to Venice, Florence, and Rome. They were traveling north again when Harry became ill. He sank rapidly through exhaustion and died on October 25.

The bitterness of the tragedy nearly broke the old man. Although Harry had never been strong, the fatal similarity of the careers of the two sons was harrowing.

This is the second blow that has fallen on me in almost the same circumstances, and just when the memory of one had been recalled and rendered familiar to all by Tennyson's remarkable volume, the Tribute of undying friendship, we are called on to lament a calamity not less bitter, and very similar in all respects. Yet not in *all*, alas! For one left behind him the living image of his talents and virtues, and seemed by the mercy of providence as it were restored in another person—while there is now nothing to fill the gap, nothing to take off the solitude of my last days, or if I have still a blessing left that prevents solitude, nothing to preserve my name and memory when I go home and am no more seen.[121]

Gladstone was in Italy at the same time learning of the iniquities of Neapolitan prison life. He met Hallam and recorded in his journal the "indescribable pain" with which he heard the news.[122] Hallam returned to England alone and, when Macaulay called on him soon after, Hallam wept.[123] Harry was buried at Clevedon beside his brother, his sister, and his mother at the end of the year. Thackeray was present at the funeral and described to Mrs. Brookfield how, as the coffin was lowered, "the dear old father . . . went down into the cave and gave the coffin a last kiss. There was no standing that last most affectionate touch of nature."[124]

Last Years

Hallam was now seventy-three. Even so, he traveled. He continued a vigorous social life. He helped to correct some of Murray's new tourist guide books.[125] In 1851 he visited Scotland and was a guest of the queen at Balmoral.[126] The following year he went abroad for the last time, visiting Guizot and his family near Lisieux in France.

Hallam's sole surviving child, Julia, married into a Kentish baronet's family in May 1852 and, in the summer of that year, Hallam went to live with them at Pickhurst, near Bromley. His domestic life was brightened by the birth, in March 1853, of twin daughters to Julia.[127]

During these years he was writing to younger historians and passing judgment on their work. In the autumn of 1851 Lord Mahon published his volumes on the mid-eighteenth century. Hallam in general approved the work though "your Chatham piety made you rather more Whiggish & American than I am, though you can never lose your impartiality." [128] He was not so gentle, however, to George Bancroft, who, having retired as minister to London in 1849, devoted himself to his vast *History of the United States* and published volumes 4 and 5 in 1852. "I must fairly tell you," Hallam wrote firmly to Bancroft on acknowledging the gift of the publication, that I do not go along with your strictures on English statesmen & on England, either in substance, or, still more, in tone. You write as an historian, but you must expect that we shall read as Englishmen. Faults there were, but I do not think all were on one side. At all events, a more moderate tone would carry more weight. An historian has the high office of holding the scales. Our friend Lord Mahon has exhibited remarkable impartiality— his last two volumes are very pleasingly written, though perhaps they drop too much into anecdote.[129]

This, though severe, was fair, for Bancroft had written, when he sent Hallam the volumes: "I have been too careful a student of your Constitutional History of England, not to have had the true model of fairness & impartial discussion before my eyes."[130]

Hallam's literary activity was not confined to commenting on the work of others. He gathered together a number of extracts from the *Literature of Europe,* and these were published by Murray in the autumn of 1852 under the title of *Literary Essays and Characters* and advertised as railway literature.

But his powers were greatly limited, when in the spring of 1854, he suffered a paralytic seizure, which led to his becoming a semi-invalid for the rest of his life.[131] Macaulay, in February 1856, found him "quite prisoner to his sofa, unable to walk. To write legibly he has long been unable."[132] Sir Henry Holland, his doctor and friend for forty years, was impressed by the effect of the illness "on him, rarely found in such cases, of diffusing a placid gentleness over the sterner qualities of the mind, . . . a mind disputative and dogmatical in its natural bent."[133] Even so, he maintained a lively interest in his surroundings. He argued the merits of the Crimean War with his nephew.[134] He tried reading George Sand but was not impressed.[135] He kept a keen eye on his financial affairs, buying up a large number of shares in the Great Western Railway Company.[136] He read the important books that were being published—Moore's *Journal,* Prescott's *Philip the Second,* Lady Holland's *Life and Letters of Sydney Smith,* and the first volume of Buckle's *History of Civilisation in England.*[137]

During these last years Hallam was frequently at home to visitors. Just before his eighty-first birthday John Lothrop Motley paid him a respectful visit and sent a vivid account to his wife. "The great historian is long past the 'middle ages' now. He is paralysed in the right leg, the right arm, and slightly in the tongue. His face is large, regularly handsome, ruddy, fresh, and very good-humoured. He received me with great cordiality, and we had half an hour's talk. . . . His mind does not seem essentially dimmed, and there is nothing senile in his aspect, crippled as he is. He is a wreck, but he has not sunk head downwards, as you sometimes see, which is the most melancholy termination to the voyage. His mind seems bright and his spirits seem light."[138]

But early in 1859 he sank fast. He died on 21 January, aged eighty-one and a half, with his family present, "without a moan or a struggle."[139]

The body was taken to Clevedon and buried a week later, the Reverend W. H. Brookfield conducting the service. A group of friends sought to perpetuate Hallam's memory, and after a five-year delay a statue seven and a half feet high was carved in marble by William Sheed, and erected on a five-foot pedestal. This was placed in the crypt of St. Paul's Cathedral, with a commemorative inscription, defiantly in English. It can be seen there today.

Chapter Two
The Middle Ages

Plan and Distribution of the Work

Hallam's first full-scale work, *View of the State of Europe during the Middle Ages,* was published in 1818. The work was begun in 1808[1]—several years before Hallam thought of writing a work on the Middle Ages. Some of the long chapter on the English Constitution was written in 1811 and in 1812.[2] The chapter on feudalism was completed in 1813.[3] Parts of the last chapter on the state of society were written in 1814, parts in 1816. The chapter on ecclesiastical power was written in 1816.[4] There are other chapters on France, Italy, Spain, Germany, and the Greek and Saracenic empires.

The work is divided into nine chapters of unequal length. Each chapter can be seen as a self-contained entity. The distribution of attention among the chapters is revealing. Hallam's insularity is reflected in the amount of space given to English history. If one includes the chapter on feudalism, which deals largely with France, the French history occupies a further fifth of the work. Compare this with four percent on Germany and two and a half percent on the Greeks and Saracens! This dispropostion is not improved by the final chapter on society which draws its examples mostly from western Europe or on ecclesiastical power which again deals only with the Roman Catholic church. The four percent on Germany is, furthermore, a pointer to the comparative ignorance of Germany and German history at this time.

Hallam and German Studies

At the turn of the century, German literature was little known in Britain. Coleridge and Scott, in their youths, studied the language and translated some of the works of modern romantic German literature. At this time Hallam was at Oxford and was struggling conscientiously with a German teacher but with little success. In the autumn of 1797 he confided in his diary: "I have acquired some knowledge of German, but not enough to enable me to read it with ease." He resolved to attack German in the following years, but in the annual review in his diary he lamented in October 1799, "The studies which I aimed to pursue last year: Chemistry, Anatomy—German have been even more neglected."[5] It seems Hallam made little more progress in German, for in the work under review he uses no German authorities for his history of Germany and in a footnote has to confess that he was "unable to judge of Müller's history in the original language." In the same work there is a remark on German scholarship that mingles awe with paternalism. "Liebnitz . . . expressed a wish that some one conversant with modern philosophy would undertake to extract the scattered particles of gold which may be hid in their abandoned mines. [Hallam is writing of the works of scholastic philosophers.] The wish has been at length partially fulfilled by three or four of those industrious students and keen metaphysicians who do honour to modern Germany."[6] Although several times in his life Hallam visited German-speaking countries he does not seem ever to have mastered the language, for in 1841 the young Henry Thomas Buckle acted as his interpreter.[7]

There is evidence, however, that he learned enough German to read. He quotes Ranke and Grimm and others in editions of his *Introduction to the Literature of Europe* and in his *Supplemental Notes to the Middle Ages*. All the time he had a distant respect for German industry, but again this was tinged with a suspicion that German scholarship may have been something of an intellectual fad. He did not appreciate the importance of Niebuhr, nor of Ranke. In 1837 he commented on Raumer's visit to England that year in a letter to his friend, Lord Mahon. "Raumer, I agree with you, has not gained much glory by his visits to England—he is a good soul but will not set the Thames on fire what conviction soever he may cause on the Spree. His fellow-professor Ranke seems much superior—but I know him only from his writings and these Germans have an instinct for history, though they may make little of the present or future."[8] This remark is interesting. History, to Hallam, is, it would appear, of little value unless it is related to the present or future. In 1837 there had been no English translation of any of Ranke's works, although Mrs. Sarah Austin was at work translating the volumes on the papacy—a translation that appeared in 1840 and was reviewed by Macaulay in the *Edinburgh Review.* There had been a French translation of the work in 1836. Hallam, therefore, must have read the French translation soon after it appeared or else have worked through the German.

By the 1840s interest in Germany and German was pervading all aspects of English life. The queen had married a German prince and a number of Teutonisms were introduced to Britain. The reorganization of the curricula at Oxford and Cambridge and the foundation of the new universities owed much to the example of German models. The reform of the civil service and the elimination of corruption in the army was partly inspired by Prussian bureaucracy. The experience of the Zollverein was used as an argument for free trade. Dr. Arnold taught German together with other modern languages at Rugby. It became as important to know German as French or Italian for the man of letters; otherwise, like Mr. Casaubon in *Middlemarch,* he would be left behind in the world of learning. But even in translation, German writers had their interpreters in England and thereby reached a wide audience. Coleridge introduced the Schlegels and Schiller to England. Carlyle had translated Goethe and found his earliest inspiration in German literature. George Eliot translated Strauss and Feuerbach. And it was not only literature and philosophy that were shaken up by German methods in the 1840s and 1850s. Theological and exegetical criticism produced some of the acutest crises of the Victorian conscience. The mid-Victorian revivalists totally ignored it. J. H. Newman boldly spurned it, but it was nervously absorbed by A. P. Stanley and the Broad Church.

Niebuhr's classical studies reached England in the 1820s. The first translation by F. A. Walter appeared in 1826 and a more scholarly edition was produced by J. C. Hare and Connop Thirlwall in 1828–32. His interest in myths and legends and his skeptical treatment of Livy had led Germans to treat in the same way not only the Bible but also medieval German history. There was a burst of interest in the German world of the Middle Ages. Germans identified the Goths with themselves, as it were, and collected all the evidence of the German past. Hence, for example, the collection of fairy tales by the philologists, the brothers Grimm. The enthusiasm spread to England and the old idea of innocent Saxon forefathers took on a new lease of life. Victorian

England saw a widespread revival of the myth of ancient Teutonic freedom, typified—if not glorified—in such historical novels as Bulwer Lytton's *Harold* (1848). To Dr. Arnold, lecturing to Oxford undergraduates in the early 1840s, the feature absent in the ancient world was the German race.

What was not there was simply the German race and the peculiar qualities which characterise it. The one addition was of such power that it changed the character of the whole-mass; the peculiar stamp of the middle ages is undoubtedly German; the change manifested in the last three centuries has been owing to the revival of older elements with great power so that the German element has been manifestly predominant. But that element still preserves its force, and is felt for good or evil in almost every country of the civilized world.[9]

The great significance and importance of the German historical movement seems to have eluded Henry Hallam. Just as he remained cool to the cult of medievalism, so he fell short in calculation of German scholarship. In the 1840s Caroline Fox recorded him as thinking that the English were "infatuated about German critics and showing it by their indiscriminate imitation of them, tasteless as he considers them."[10]

Spain and Greece in Hallam's Work

It is noteworthy, too, that Spain occupied more space than Germany in Hallam's history. Interest in Spain intensified during the Peninsular War. Southey's work, as Hallam himself recognized,[11] interpreted the Iberian countries to Englishmen who, after the Convention of Cintra of 1808, saw the cause of Spain as their own. It was in 1808 that Hallam showed his colors by learning Spanish.[12] Hallam, moreover, saw in the constitutional development of Castile and Aragon in the Middle Ages many parallels with the English constitution under the Plantagenets.

The dozen or so pages on the Greek and Saracenic empires are significant. In his view of Byzantine history, Hallam followed Gibbon closely, thereby reflecting contemporary tastes. Interest in the Greek cause was based on sympathies with Greece's classical past. It was not until the 1840s that Englishmen began to see Byzantium as anything

more than a tragic epilogue to classical civilization. The attitudes of
Englishmen were changed by two men above others: George Finlay and
John Mason Neale. Finlay was a veteran of the Greek War of Independence and settled on an estate in Attica. From 1844 to 1861 he published
his *History of Greece*. He was one of the first philhellenes to concentrate
on the Byzantine period and his works were eagerly publicized by E. A.
Freeman. Neale's motivation for interpreting the history of medieval
Greece was theological. He was a keen supporter of the Tractarian
movement and became a leader of the Anglo-Catholic revival. He found
in the Greek church a medieval opponent of Rome that was in no way
Protestant and that possessed all the beauty of holiness in hymns,
poetry, liturgy, and ritual. From the 1840s he wrote much on the
Eastern church and its history, translated medieval Greek works of
devotion and even wrote a novel on the fall of Constantinople.

Definition of the Middle Ages

Hallam's work was one of the first major historical works to use the
phrase "the Middle Ages." The expression has been traced back to the
seventeenth century and is clearly a post-Renaissance concept, referring
to the gap between the civilizations of Greece and Rome and of
"modern" Europe. The concept of the Middle Ages, indeed, contains in
itself the concept of the Renaissance. But the idea of the Middle Ages
assumed a definition and a clarity as an epoch long before the Renaissance did. This was probably because of the polemical implications of
the term. Ideas may vary about the timing of the end of the Middle
Ages, but it is clear that one factor absent from the Middle Ages was
organized Protestantism on a national basis. The Middle Ages, consequently, was an emotionally charged term and an issue in theological
controversy.

What did Hallam mean by the Middle Ages? In the last chapter of
the work, he wrote that the division he adopted comprised "about a
thousand years, from the invasion of France by Clovis to that of Naples
by Charles VIII." But in his introduction, he was less categorical not
only about the terminal points but also about the validity of periodiza-
tion. "The continuous chain of transactions on the stage of human
society is ill-divided by mere links of chronological demarcation."
Although the terminal points that he unwillingly adopts in the preface
and more assertively states in the body of the work are political events,

they are to Hallam convenient points that mark the division of ancient, medieval, and modern history. The "subversion of the western empire is manifestly the natural termination of ancient history," and was, presumably, with equal naturalness, the beginning of the Middle Ages. Yet this *political* event reflected a more fundamental social and intellectual change. "Law neglected, philosophy perverted until it became contemptible, history nearly silent, art more and more violated; such were the symptoms by which the age previous to Constantine announced the decline of human intellect." Yet terminal points brought on difficulties. Venice dated "from an era beyond the commencement of the middle ages." Was Venice an ancient or a medieval state? This problem is acuter in dealing with Byzantium. "In tracing the long series of Byzantine annals, we never lose sight of antiquity."[13]

A similar problem faced Hallam at the end of the Middle Ages. He seems to want to represent the end by an identifiable event. Yet, at the same time, he realized that the world does not change overnight and that the change of epochs can take generations. In 1808, in reviewing Coxe's *House of Austria,* Hallam had asserted with uncharacteristic assurance that the accession of Maximilian was "the precise point where the twilight of the middle ages terminates, and the sunshine of modern history commences."[14] Ten years later, the end of the Middle Ages is seen as a far more gradual process. "We begin in darkness and calamity; and, though the shadows grow fainter as we advance, yet we are to break off our pursuit as the morning breathes upon us, and the twilight reddens into the lustre of day." The end of the fifteenth century is to Hallam the most convenient point to mark the end of this twilight, though there are differences in different countries that "naturally terminate the history of the middle ages": events such as the Diet of Worms in Germany, the accession of the Tudors in England, the fall of Constantinople in the Eastern Mediterranean. But "the invasion of Naples by Charles VIII was the event that first engaged the principal states in relations of alliance or hostility which may be deduced to the present day, and is the point at which every man who traces backwards its political history will be obliged to pause." In short, for Hallam as for Robertson, half a century earlier, the beginning of modern history is characterized by the start of systems of balance of power.

Similarly, a cultural improvement also marks the beginning of modern history. All countries sank into barbarism after the fall of the Roman Empire in the west, but the nadir was reached in different countries at different times. "France reached her lowest point at the beginning of the eighth century; but England was at that time more respectable, and did not fall into complete degradation till the middle of the ninth." There is seen a steady improvement that finally breaks out into modern European civilization. In support of this improvement Hallam speaks of "the natural tendency of mankind to ameliorate their condition," a tendency manifest most notably in the progress of the English constitution; yet elsewhere he is skeptical about this tendency to improvement. He draws contrasts from different countries and centuries in order to illustrate comparative improvement, yet he is even here cautious about such a method.

In comparing . . . the fifteenth with the twelfth century, no-one would deny the vast increase of navigation and manufactures, the superior refinement of manners, the greater diffusion of literature. But should I assert that man had raised himself above the moral degradation of a more barbarous age, I might be met with the question, whether history bears witness to any greater excesses of rapine and inhumanity than in the wars of France and England under Charles VII, or whether the rough patriotism and fervid passions of the Lombards in the twelfth century were not better than the systematic treachery of their servile descendants three hundred years afterwards.[15]

Medieval Barbarism and Ignorance

Hallam had little time for a detailed study of the early Middle Ages. In his first published review, in 1805, the details of sixth- and seventh-century France were scorned. "The annals of these princes are ineffably wearisome and uninstructive," he wrote. "Whether the Offas and the Pendas, the Chilperics and the Dagoberts, had a vice more or less, we have as little solicitude to enquire, as about any question which the busy demon of controversy can possibly suggest."[16] But such remarks, reminiscent of Hume and of the Age of Reason, became less acceptable as the nineteenth century advanced. Indeed, a collation of successive editions of the *Middle Ages* reveals a progressive moderation of the more vituperative examples of rationalist scorn. For example, a remark in the first edition on the Goths in Spain—"I hold the annals of barbarians so unworthy of remembrance that I will not detain the reader by naming one sovereign of that obscure race"—becomes in later editions—"I will not detain the reader by naming one sovereign of that obscure race." The need to record "worth" or "profit" in a fact leads Hallam to remark on early medieval France: "it is a weary and unprofitable task to follow these changes in detail, through scenes of tumult and bloodshed, in which the eye meets with no sunshine, nor can rest on any interesting spot." It is as if facts were themselves moral agents, to be applauded or rejected or considered worthy of interest. "History," Hallam wrote apologetically, "which reflects only the more prominent features of society, cannot exhibit the virtues that were scarcely able to struggle through the general depravation."[17]

When Hallam is explicit about the barbarism and depravity of the Middle Ages, he refers repeatedly to the ignorance of the clergy and their dominant role in society. He notes that even the church recognized the ignorance of the clergy which, in almost every council, "forms a subject for reproach." He is skeptical about the contribution of the clergy to learning. He does concede that the preservation of "a few sparks of ancient learning" was due to the "establishment of Christianity. Religion alone made a bridge, as it were, across the chaos, and linked the two periods of ancient and modern civilisation." But the preservation of ancient works was often a matter of chance, for in the libraries of monasteries, "the far greater part of the books were monastic trash"; palimpsests, for example, "occasioned probably the loss of many ancient authors, who have made way for the legends of saints and other ecclesiastical rubbish." Monasticism in itself was harmful to the cause of learning.

The torrent of irrational superstitions which carried all before it in the fifth century, and the process of ascetic enthusiasm had an influence still more decidedly inimical to learning. I cannot indeed conceive any state of society more adverse to the intellectual improvement of mankind than one which admitted of no middle line between gross dissoluteness and fanatical mortification. . . . After the introduction of monkery and its unsocial theory of duties, . . . it might be a difficult question, whether the cultivators and admirers of useful literature were less likely to be found among the profligate citizens of Rome and their barbarian conquerors, or the melancholy recluses of the wilderness.

This general ignorance, which resulted from the alienation of the cultivated, led to superstition. "In the shadows of this universal ignorance, a thousand superstitions, like foul animals of the night, were propagated and nourished." And this superstition helped to strengthen the authority of the church and clergy. "Men were infatuated enough to surrender themselves, as well as their properties, to churches and monasteries, in return for such benefit as they might reap by the prayers of their new masters." This domination of the clergy, Hallam saw as a pagan survival. The gods of the woods were abandoned, "but they retained the elementary principles of that worship and of all barbarous idolatry, a superstitious reverence for the priesthood, a credulity that served and invited imposture, and a confidence in the efficacy of gifts to expiate offences." Hallam was further offended by what he saw as the intolerance and bigotry of medieval religion. He is generous in his appreciation of St. Louis who was, however, impressed "with a belief in the duty of exterminating all enemies to the faith." Intolerance was a product of enthusiasm which was "little else than superstition put in motion. . . . Nor has any denomination of Christians produced, or even sanctioned, more fanaticism, than the church of Rome."[18]

Hallam's Treatment of the Crusades

A sustained example of everything that was superstitious, intolerant, and fanatical was the Crusades. In his treatment of this period, Hallam is similar to his eighteenth-century predecessors—Robertson, Hume, Gibbon—but there are some striking and characteristic deviations.

The treatment of the Crusades around 1800 was tied up with one's view of the contemporary world. Protestants found it difficult to approve of an enterprise undertaken by the pope. The men of the Enlightenment—Voltaire, for example, or Hume—found the Crusaders full of mixed motives, many of them unworthy. Gibbon saw the movement as somewhat absurd. It was only with the romantics that the Crusades were in favor, especially in France. Napoleon's Egyptian expedition was seen as an echo of Louis's Egyptian expedition and inspired Michaud and Chateaubriand to view the Crusades with greater sympathy.[19] Hallam's approach to the Crusades is philosophical: that is to say, he resists a narrative and discusses them as a problem rather than as a fact. It is clear all the time that he does not approve of the enterprises and sees unworthy motives in many of the participants. And yet he concedes that religious enthusiasm was the prime motivation and he thus differs from the rationalist historians "incapable of sympathizing with the blind fervour of zeal." In arguing against these historians, he invokes contemporary evidence and the improbability of their position. Men in the eleventh and twelfth centuries—even the princes—lacked the "refinements" to be any other than religiously motivated: in other words, the Crusades were an outcome of the barbarous times. And, again, he writes of Louis surviving "the spirit of the crusades" as if, somehow, the Crusades had a spirit and laws of their own. This is the embryo of an historicism that was not confined to Hallam alone in 1818.[20] Hints of this occur elsewhere in Hallam's work. The Crusades were what they were because the times were what they were. But Hallam retains enough of the eighteenth-century approach to see a futility in the whole operation.

Another distinction in his treatment of the Crusades is in the small part he allows the papacy to have played. Indeed, the section on the Crusades occurs in the chapter on France rather than the chapter on ecclesiastical power, for the very secular reason that Frenchmen were principally involved in the campaigns.[21] His disapproval of the church of Rome is reserved for the chapter on "Ecclesiastical Power."

The Church as a Political Institution

Attitudes to saints, shrines, miracles, and the Blessed Virgin Mary and doctrines such as the infallibility of the church, the intercessory power of Mary and the saints, and transubstantiation were common both to the medieval church and to nineteenth-century Roman Catholicism. Thus even a liberal Protestant like Hallam was not always able to distinguish the two. Hallam had been an active writer on behalf of emancipation of the Roman Catholics. His liberalism did not suggest any warmth, however, toward the Roman position past or present. In 1805 he had written about the Reformation in the *Edinburgh Review*.

How greatly has it helped to diffuse the light of reason and how much has it contributed towards the restoration of true philosophy! What nests of vice and idleness were destroyed with the monasteries! The Reformation put a stop to the unjust encroachments of the ecclesiastical on the civil power. It banished for ever a thousand superstitions. Through it, Great Britain ceased to be drained of its wealth by foreign priests; and the mendicants, who were

fed from the table of lazy monks and pampered abbots, have been succeeded
by useful artisans and industrious labourers. Instead of convents, we now
build manufactories; instead of the images of saints, we display the contents
of our warehouses; and instead of crowns of martyrdom, we hear of the laurels
won by the brave defenders of their country's glory.[22]

There is much evidence that this harsh view of Roman Catholicism
softened during Hallam's life. His scornful Protestant feeling is not so
bitter in 1818, though in the *Middle Ages* he sees the ecclesiastical
history as "one long contention of fraud against robbery."[23] But
remarks and asides that might have been regarded as offensive to
Roman Catholics were toned down in later editions. For example, in
later editions, he honors Dunstan with the addition of "Saint" which he
had omitted in the 1818 edition. Oddly enough, John Lingard in his
History had avoided calling Dunstan "Saint" in order to gain the
readership of Protestants.[24] And some of Hallam's liberal remarks on
morals in Roman Catholic countries in the *Constitutional History* roused
Robert Southey to Protestant rage.

But theological disapproval is never far away in his view of the
medieval church. He was apt to see papal authority in no other light
than that of a political institution with feudal claims and absolute
tendencies. Its spiritual authority was an "imposture . . . too palpable
for any but the most ignorant to credit."[25] Throughout the work,
Hallam approaches ecclesiastical and religious problems in a frame of
mind similar to that in which he approached political problems. The
mystique is stripped away. He considers the reality of power in a liberal,
utilitarian and empirical temper. Even the language of politics is used.

The medieval church, according to Hallam, grew rich in the early
Middle Ages by means both fair and foul. After the fifth century
"covetousness, especially, became almost a characteristic vice." As the
richest archbishopric, Rome "became a prey to the most terrible
disorders: the papal chair was sought at best by bribery, or controlling
influence, often by violence and assassination: it was filled by such men
as naturally rise by such means, whose sway was precarious, and
generally ended either in their murder or degradation." Gregory VII
purified the papacy, but at the same time his claims to authority
exhibited "an arrogance without parallel, and an ambition that grasped
at universal and unlimited monarchy." The despotism in 1245 of
Frederick II was "the most pompous act of usurpation in all the records

of the church of Rome: and the tacit approbation of a general council seemed to incorporate the pretended right of deposing Kings, which might have passed as a mad vaunt of Gregory VII and his successors, with the established faith of Christendom." Spiritual weapons were used in personal conflicts, such as excommunication and canonization—the former "were issued on every provocation rather as a weapon of ecclesiastical warfare"; the latter was "a reward which the church has always held out to its most active friends, and which may be compared to titles of nobility granted by a temporal sovereign." In the central Middle Ages Hallam sees a progression of audacity in the persons who were popes. "As Gregory VII appears the most usurping of mankind till we read the history of Innocent III, so Innocent III is thrown into shade by the superior audacity of Boniface VIII." The successors of Innocent III "aspired to render every European Kingdom formally dependent upon the see of Rome"; and it was Boniface VIII who declared "the subjection of every human being to the see of Rome to be an article of faith."[26]

To these claims of Gregory, Innocent and Boniface there grew up an opposition among the laity "which ripened into an alienation of sentiment from the Church; and a condition of that sacred truth, which superstition and sophistry have endeavoured to eradicate from the heart of men, that no tyrannical government can be founded on a divine commission." This "sacred truth" and the fierceness with which it is stated suggests that Hallam has other regimes nearer home in mind. The suspicion is confirmed when one notes his treatment of the Conciliar movement, which aimed at making councils the final authority of the church instead of the pope. The Conciliar movement displayed what he calls "the whig principles of the church." By this he means a constitutional control and check on monarchist and absolutist tendencies of the papacy. He also approves the Gallican church, and, commenting on the decrees of the Council of Constance, proclaiming the authority of councils, he writes that they "are the great pillars of that moderate theory with respect to papal authority which distinguished the Gallican Church, and is embraced, I presume, by almost all laymen and the major part of ecclesiastics on this side of the Alps. They embarrass the more popish churchmen, as the Revolution does our English Tories."[27] Regard for these Whig principles of the councillors of Constance does not inhibit Hallam from condemning their treatment of Hus; Hallam never suffered from an excess of reverence.

Hallam and Catholic Historians

In another part of his work, Hallam draws a contrast between the practice of the Roman church of his day and of the heat of its historical writing. Frederick II is still the cause of rancor, and Giannone "suffered for his boldness" in drawing that monarch too favorably. "Although," Hallam goes on, "the public policy of Rome has long displayed the pacific temper of weakness, the thermometer of ecclesiastical sentiment in that city stands very nearly as high as in the 13th century." He scorns Catholic historians as a breed and is wary of their enthusiasm for medieval "civilisation." "A proneness to extoll every monk, of whose production a few letters or a devotional treatise survives, every bishop, of whom it is related that he composed homilies, runs through the laborious work of the Benedictines of St. Maur." Similarly, he warns against translating admiration for medieval cathedrals into an affection for the period. "These structures uniting sublimity in general composition with the beauties of variety and form, intricacy of parts, skilful or at least fortunate effects of shadow and light, and in some instances with extraordinary mechanical science, are naturally apt to lead those antiquaries who are most conversant with them into too partial estimates of the times wherein they are founded."[28]

What Hallam disliked in Catholic historians was their glorification of priestly authority. Such glorification led him to be persistently bitter to High Church historians and principles. "It ought always to be remembered, that *ecclesiastical,* and not merely papal, encroachments are what civil governments and the laity in general have had to keep out of sight. . . . The true enemy is what are called High Church principles: be they maintained by a pope, a bishop, or a presbyter."[29]

However, Hallam was able to see the merits of the work of John Lingard, whom he reviewed very favorably in the *Edinburgh Review* in 1831. The review was in some ways a restitution, first, for some sharp words in the *Middle Ages*; and second, for a scathing review of earlier volumes of Lingard's *History* in the *Edinburgh Review* by the Holland House physician, Dr. John Allen. Hallam was reviewing the last two volumes of Lingard's work. In the world of the 1830s and 1840s, Hallam and Lingard were survivors from the eighteenth century. They both deplored the excesses of the new Catholicism and the new Protestantism and, curiously enough, had much in common. Both were old-fashioned Whigs. Both were friends of Henry Brougham, contemporary polymath, a controversial and disturbing figure. Hallam supported and advocated the repeal of the penal laws, and Lingard was happy to escape from the siege atmosphere of pre-Emancipation English Catholicism. Both had a similar contempt for the enthusiasm and the spiritual gymnastics of some of the adherents of the Oxford movement. These two men, who both lived from the 1770s to the 1850s, had a similar purpose in the writing of history. Hallam aimed at an impartiality that would transcend parties, even though this "impartiality" was naturally restricted by his definition of it and of Hallam's own circumstances. Lingard aimed to write a history that Protestants would read.[30]

Providence

It would be expected that a providential interpretation of history would not have appealed to Hallam. This is not so. Perhaps a century of rationalism had made the issue of providence more irrelevant than it had been in the days of Bossuet. Yet Hallam occasionally invokes Providence to explain otherwise inexplicable events. Providence appears, as one would expect, always on the side of Hallam's sympathies. Providence was a Whig. It is possible that the Napoleonic Wars had partly restored Providence to favor. Against very great odds, Britain managed to curb the limitless ambitions of Napoleon. Was this, it was asked, not a sure sign that God was on "our" side? Such a man as Dr. Arnold said so quite categorically when he lectured to his Oxford audience as Regius Professor in 1841.[31]

Hallam, too, saw the working of Providence in the Napoleonic Wars, and in comments on medieval history he hints at this. When Charles VIII of France crushed Ludovico Sforza who sought to usurp the dukedom of Milan, Hallam commented "It is the will of Providence, that the highest and surest wisdom, even in matters of policy, should never be unconnected with virtue." Providence, it is implied, worked against the excessive power of the papacy. "There is a spell wrought by uninterrupted good fortune," said Hallam, alluding more directly to recent European history, "which captivates men's understanding and persuades them, against reasoning and analogy, that violent power is immortal and irresistible." Even more explicitly, the moral is drawn from the defeat of Barbarossa in northern Italy. "Providence reserves to itself various means, by which the bonds of the oppressor may be broken: and it is not for human sagacity to anticipate whether the army of a conqueror shall moulder in the unwholesome marshes of Rome, or stiffen with frost in a Russian winter."[32]

Hallam's Approach to Church History

Providence is, according to Hallam, independent of human institutions. This emphasizes the interest of the chapter on "Ecclesiastical Power." The title is highly significant. It is not "The Church" or "Medieval Christianity." Instead it refers to something as political as "power." In the chapter, there is no attempt to understand what people in the Middle Ages believed or what the churchmen preached. There is no explanation of the development of Catholic doctrine or liturgy; no explanation of the vocation of the religious; no sympathetic understanding of, say, St. Francis. In spite of these limitations, Hallam is making a considerable advance in the history of historiography. The matters which Hallam omits were often issues of ecclesiastical polemics and theological controversy. Ecclesiastical history was not often the subject of a layman. But Hallam followed Gibbon, as Gibbon followed Voltaire, "in boldly sweeping away every barrier between sacred history and profane history."[33]

The history of Christendom is not seen as the working out of God's purpose. It has a social significance, and affects and is affected by contemporary circumstances. He was not concerned, he said, with the "erroneousness" of medieval religion; "but its effect upon the moral and intellectual character of mankind was so prominent, that no-one can take a philosophical view of the middle ages without attending more than is at present fashionable to their ecclesiastical history." "A calm, comprehensive study of ecclesiastical history," he wrote elsewhere, "is an antidote to extravagant apprehensions." It was of great value in considering Europe apart from the traditional framework. "It is an advantageous circumstance," he wrote in the conclusion to his chapter on ecclesiastical power, "for the philosophical enquirer into the history of ecclesiastical dominion, that, as it spreads itself over the vast extent of fifteen centuries, the dependence of events upon general causes, rather than on transitory combinations of the character of individuals, is made more evident."[34]

Approach to Medieval English Constitutional History

"No unbiased observer, who derives pleasure from the welfare of his species, can fail to consider the long and uninterruptedly increasing prosperity of England as the most beautiful phenomenon in the history of mankind."[35]

With these words, Henry Hallam introduced his chapter on the constitutional history of England in the Middle Ages. The words, published in a year of distress, the year before Peterloo, are offensively complacent, but they state the key of the chapter, the theme of Hallam's view of English history, and, in some way, serve as a redeeming justification for an excessively long chapter. In this chapter Hallam avoided giving a narrative. He also avoided credulity, cynicism, or paternalism in his attitude to England's medieval past. His interest in the subject does not lead him to make great claims for the medieval constitution. At the same time his "philosophy" does not make him dismiss the significance of the development of the constitution. In his concern for institutional development, based on sound evidence, he resembles William Stubbs. In his skepticism about the legalistic seventeenth-century interpretations of the Norman Conquest or the origin of parliament, he is akin to Robert Brady and David Hume. His combination of Whiggism and "philosophy" was the pattern for most nineteenth-century writers on the constitution. His framework of interpretation was, with individual variations, basically that also of Freeman, J. R. Green, Stubbs, and F. W. Maitland.

Anglo-Saxon Liberties and the Norman Conquest

Pre-Conquest history is dealt with sketchily. Hallam clearly did not see this period as of much importance in the history of the constitution. Anglo-Saxon liberties had been an issue of controversy in the seventeenth century. The historiography of the following century, however, represents a watershed between the legalistic concern for pre-Conquest history and a romantic revival of nostalgia for a mythical golden age. The indications of belief in this golden age, broken by the Conquest, were few and were of significance only as straws in the wind or as statements of a political program. The anonymous author of an *Historical Essay on the English Constitution* in 1771 believed that the constitution existed in a complete form with liberties safeguarded in 450 A.D.

Jefferson and Wilkes both professed an enthusiasm for the Anglo-Saxons and a belief in this primitive freedom had a vogue for a generation among radical writers.[36] But among historians there was much agreement about the small relevance of Anglo-Saxon studies to constitutional development. Hallam would have agreed with Hume's statement that "the great body even of the free citizens, in those ages, really enjoyed much less true liberty than where the execution of the laws is most severe, and where subjects are reduced to the strictest subordination and dependence on the civil magistrate."[37]

The Norman Conquest has to the present day been an issue of almost emotional controversy.[38] The "Conquest" is, of course, the reverse side of the coin of Anglo-Saxon liberty. An idea has persisted for many centuries that somehow the Saxons were on the side of freedom and that feudalism, introduced by William, represented a new powerful landed aristocracy, authority, and Toryism. Throughout the nineteenth century the Norman Conquest was a theme for novels and plays. Although their authors—Kingsley, Lytton, Tennyson—projected the nineteenth century into these fictional accounts, Victorian writing on the Conquest lacked the political urgency that occurs in the writers of the seventeenth century.[39] Then, parliamentary antiquarians had been anxious to argue a continuity of the constitution; accordingly, the Conquest had to be explained away or interpreted as irrelevant to the progress of the constitution. To concede a Conquest was to surrender power to a king, a dangerous precedent in the age of Charles I and James II. Coke and his successors, both the opponents and defenders of royal supremacy, argued that the Norman kings swore to uphold the laws of Edward the Confessor. Once this was demonstrated, then the sovereignty of the law was maintained.

After 1700 the urgency of this approach was becoming irrelevant. It was no longer necessary to discuss the Conquest as a precedent that had direct application to the present. The change—as in much of the developments of modern interpretations of medieval history—can be seen as early as Sir Henry Spelman. Brady, at the end of the century, developed the hints of Spelman. The clue to this new view of history was the discovery of feudalism. Brady, as Pocock has said, "built up the first thorough reconstruction of feudal society as a thing existing wholly in the past and intelligible only on its principles."[40] After 1688 and even more so after 1714 there were no longer bitter historical controversies on the nature of sovereignty. The answers to present political problems were not necessarily to be found in past precedents, although examples from the past might reinforce theories of the present.

Hallam, like the historians of the eighteenth century, had no worries about admitting a conquest or conceding that feudalism was introduced by William I. He is in the long historiographical watershed between the seventeenth-century antiquarians and the nineteenth-century Teutonists. David Hume had stated bluntly that in 1066 "England of a sudden became a feudal kingdom." William was a conqueror; his intentions were hostile and he acted as a master. "It is evident that the present rights and privileges of the people, who are a mixture of English and Normans, can never be affected by a transaction which passed seven hundred years ago."[41] And Hallam, like Hume, disdains as irrelevant the controversy of what he calls Normans and anti-Normans.[42]

In his treatment of William I, Hallam admits the historical argument of Brady, but seems keen to preserve a vestige of the anti-Brady argument. According to Hallam, William was offered the English crown in accordance with, perhaps the promise, certainly the intentions, of Edward the Confessor. The assent of the people was given and William's accession was as regular "as the circumstances of the times would permit." Nonetheless, the Norman kings imposed a tyranny. "The exclusion of the English from political privileges was accompanied with such a confiscation of property as never perhaps has proceeded from any government not avowedly founding its title upon the sword." Hallam seems to say that effectively there was a conquest, but there is also a strong hint that there was a political continuity. And there is a similar ambivalence in his verdict on Norman government. On the other hand, William permitted "no rapine but his own"; and this, on the other hand, did ensure external peace and "the security that the English found from invasion on the side of Denmark and Norway."[43]

Feudalism, too, was not suddenly introduced. Some of its features were only gradually brought in and later received the force of law. Hallam here again clings to the echo of "ancient liberty." In his chapter on feudalism, he is careful to distinguish English from continental feudalism. The Norman system was "restrained by regular legislation, by paramount courts, by justice, by learned writings, from breaking into discordant local usages, except in a comparatively small number of places, and has become the principal source of our common law." But this is strongly qualified in the chapter on the English constitution, by a caution against certainty at this time—"so unfixed, or rather unformed, were all constitutional principles."[44]

Magna Carta

To Hallam Magna Carta is the first statement of constitutionalism. "As this was the first effort towards a legal government, so is it beyond comparison the most important event in our history, except that Revolution without which its benefits would rapidly have been annihilated . . . and if every subsequent law were to be swept away, there would still remain the bold features that distinguish a free from a despotic monarchy." The provisions that are most important are "those which protect the personal liberty and property of all freemen, by giving security from arbitrary imprisonment and arbitrary spoliation."[45] In restoring Magna Carta to the center of his appreciation of the constitution, Hallam is rejecting some skepticism that crept into the accounts of some eighteenth-century historians.

To Hume Magna Carta was, it is true, the statement of "the great objects for which political society was first founded by man"; yet the motives of the barons were mixed. Magna Carta was as much in the interests of the barons as of the rest of the country: there was no guarantee, furthermore, that the nominal concessions to "the people" could be enforced.[46] John Millar went further. He wrote that the parties concerned in the negotiations for Magna Carta "were not actuated by the most liberal principles; . . . it was not so much their intention to secure the liberties of the people at large as to establish the privileges of a few individuals. A great tyrant on the one side, and a set of petty tyrants on the other seem to have divided the kingdom."[47] But Hallam restored the honorable role of the barons and, in particular, William, earl of Pembroke, and Stephen Langton, archbishop of Canterbury. To their "temperate zeal for a legal government" England was indebted for the establishment of civil liberty on an immovable basis. Hallam concedes the possible doubtful motives of some of the barons. But the fact of Magna Carta is greater than the character of some of its makers.

There were no doubts about Magna Carta in the nineteenth century after Hallam. Stubbs follows Hallam so closely that his words at times echo those of Hallam. Hallam wrote, "In this just solicitude for the people, and in the moderation, which infringed upon no essential prerogatives of the monarchy, we may perceive a liberality and patriotism very unlike the selfishness which is sometimes rashly imputed to those ancient barons." Stubbs said, "The Great Charta was won by men who were maintaining, not the cause of a class . . . but the cause of a nation." To Hallam, Magna Carta was "the first effort towards a legal government." To Stubbs, "The Great Charter is the first great public act of the nation." And for Hallam, "all that has since been obtained is little more than a confirmation or commentary"; for Stubbs, "the whole of the constitutional history of England is little more than a commentary on Magna Carta."[48] And in more popular historiography Magna Carta was treated with pious adulation. John Richard Green "found it impossible to gaze without reverence on the earliest monument of English freedom which we can see with our own eyes and touch with our own hands, the great charter, to which from age to age patriots have looked back as the basis of English liberty."[49]

The Thirteenth and Fourteenth Centuries

After Magna Carta, Hallam sees a paradox in the reign of Henry III. Public liberty might have been crushed if an abler king had followed John. But, during these centuries, principles that are enunciated in 1215 take root. Magna Carta becomes a fixed feature of the constitution and successive kings are obliged to confirm it. "The Great Charter was always considered as a fundamental law." One of the new principles established during Henry's reign was what Hallam calls "that correspondence between supply and redress, which for some centuries was the balance-spring of our constitution."[50] A further feature is that the monarchy becomes hereditary. Before the thirteenth century there had been no clear line of succession and disputes had arisen. But in the years before 1272 there is no doubt as to who the heir is, and, on Henry's death, Edward I is declared king even though he is in Sicily.

Furthermore, in the thirteenth century, there is undoubtedly a limited monarchy: the powers of the king are limited by law. The contemporary enunciation of the doctrine of a limited monarchy does not mean that the monarch refrained from disregarding these limits, but "whatever things . . . it was asserted that the king might do, it was a necessary implication that there were other things that he could not do: else it were vain to specify the former."[51] This argument is the kernel of the chapter. A declaration of limited monarchy was irreversible. Its very existence confounds any argument for legal unlimited monarchy. The rest of the chapter deals with the working out of a formula for fixing the constitution on these principles.

England, too, Hallam argues, is implicitly a democracy in the thirteenth century. There is no noble class. Only the men who have peerages are nobles. Their descendants do not all, automatically, become noble. The smaller nobility were pressed to act with the people. This factor, together with the survival of pride in local and democratic jurisdiction, was of great importance for all the centuries after the thirteenth. "It is, I am firmly persuaded, to this peculiarly democratic character of the English monarchy that we are indebted for its long permanence, its regular improvement, and its present vigour." Hallam was mindful of the troubles of Europe since 1789, and just as Macaulay reflected in 1848 that the Glorious Revolution was a providential safeguard against the disturbances that afflicted Europe in that year, so Hallam thought it a providential circumstance that "our ancestors, deviating from the usages of neighbouring countries, should, as if deliberately, have guarded against that expansive force, which, in bursting through obstacles improvidently opposed, has scattered havoc over Europe."[52]

The Origins of Parliament

The third, long part of Hallam's chapter is about the period 1272 to 1485 in the making of the constitution.[53] During this time Hallam saw the English government defining itself and the appearance of all modern liberties. The core of the two centuries is the three reigns of Richard II, Henry IV, and Henry V. There is, more or less for the first time, a narrative history of the reign of Richard II, and the lengthy discussions on the nature of parliament and the medieval government allude to the two later reigns as the time when parliament attained its legal sovereignty. The deposition of Richard is seen as a statement of the limitations of monarchy and as a valuable precedent for 1688. After 1422 the constitution becomes blurred. There is a discussion on the infancy and incapacity of Henry VI and the consequent lessons on regency. But the Wars of the Roses were a period of rapine and, like the Civil War two centuries later, furnished few useful lessons.

A discussion on the emergence of parliament and the composition of the House of Commons precedes the narrative of Richard's reign. Before Robert Brady's *Complete History of England* (1685–1700) the principal writers on the antiquities of the English constitution were lawyers, and the case for parliamentary sovereignty was maintained by asserting that precedents for Parliament's existence were declaratory of its existence from time immemorial, independent of royal control. Unfortunately there was no evidence for the existence of parliament, with a House of Commons based on borough as well as county representation, before 1265. Parliamentarians asserted that this did not deny the existence of earlier parliaments. Indeed, in the mental framework of seeing a precedent as a declaration of the law which is absolute and perennial, the evidence of 1265 pointed to an immemorial parliament with such representation. However, Brady's work upset the nature of these arguments. Brady was a physician and not a lawyer and he wrote his history to vindicate royal supremacy. But he used a new kind of common law argument, that, in fact, invalidated the whole legal-historical approach to contemporary politics. Parliament did not exist before 1265. Why should there have been a parliament before then? Parliament was a product of the feudal society of the thirteenth century, the result of special historical circumstances. Brady thus showed that "the whole cult of immemorial law was bound up with the fallacy of anachronism."[54] Although Brady was personally discredited after 1688—as a royal physician he attested the birth of the Old Pretender[55]—his work was an enormous advance in medieval scholarship. His argument about parliament's origins was irrefutable both on the old legalistic ground that he had incidentally undermined and also on the historical grounds of parliament's connection with the feudal society of the thirteenth century.

In the eighteenth century, controversy on the sovereignty of parliament was settled. The king was relatively weak and the case for parliamentary power needed no antiquarian argument to buttress it. Parliamentary sovereignty was furthermore justified by utilitarian

Lockeian arguments. Hallam is the first major English Whig historian
to consider Brady's historical arguments.

While accepting Brady's conclusion, Hallam insinuates evidence for
a belief in a regular parliament before 1265. For example, he quotes
complaints of the burgesses of St. Albans in 1315 that, according to
ancient custom, they should be represented; and the petition of the
borough of Barnstaple in 1345 claimed that "among the franchises
granted to them by a charter of Athelstan they had ever since exercised
the right of sending two burgesses to parliament." However, in positive
assertion, Hallam goes no further than to say that "the representation of
the commons in parliament was not treated as a novelty even in times
little posterior to those in which we have been supposing it to have
originated." There is thus no frontal assault on Brady. On the other
hand, throughout the *Middle Ages* there are frequent remarks impugn-
ing Brady's integrity, and the effect of these remarks is to undermine
confidence in Brady's authority. For example, Brady's "unfairness always keeps pace with his ability." Prynne's and Brady's "disposition to
narrow the basis of the constitution is so strong that it created a sort of
prejudice against their authority." Brady's *History of Boroughs* is "a work
which, if read with due suspicion of the author's honesty, will convey a
great deal of knowledge."[56]

For Hallam, "the essential principles of our constitution were fixed"
in the reign of Edward III.[57] These essential principles were the
concurrence of the two Houses of Parliament in a change of law; the
illegality of raising money without the consent of the House of Commons; and the right of the Commons to inquire into public abuses and
to impeach. During this reign, moreover, Hallam discerns the definition of a statute: its distinction from an ordinance; and its development
from a petition. After the strong rule of Edward III, the constitution
was tested under Richard II and its principles were at stake. In spite of
the king they ultimately triumphed with the accession of Henry IV.
Hence the importance of Richard's reign.

The Reign of Richard II

In the treatment of the reign of Richard II an important historiographical conflict can be seen between Hallam and David Hume. In the
treatment of earlier reigns Hallam conceded much of the "Tory"

conclusion while offering "Whig" evidence. But this reign was a reign of controversy. It had relevance to the events of 1649 and 1688. Eighteenth-century historians frequently saw the fourteenth century reflected in the seventeenth, and the historical interpretation of the former depended on the political sympathies transferred to the latter. David Hume, however, ostensibly rejects this analogy. "All the circumstances of this event [the deposition of Richard] compared to those which attended the late revolution in 1688 show the difference between a great and civilised nation, deliberately vindicating its established privileges: and a turbulent and barbarous aristocracy, plunging headlong from the extremes of one faction into those of another."[58] There was, he maintained, a case for arbitrary royal power in the 1390s. "If the king had possessed no arbitrary powers, while all the nobles assumed and exercised them, there must have ensued an absolute anarchy in the state." But in writing of the duke of Gloucester, Hume seems to be writing of a Whig of Charles II's reign—Shaftesbury perhaps. The other great historian of the eighteenth century was Thomas Carte. Carte was less influential, less attractive, and less intelligent than Hume. He does not discuss the deposition of Richard at any length. His Toryism appears only in the narrative, in the use of emotive language and damning character sketches—one feels again that he is writing of politicians nearer his own day. Carte contrasts Richard— "the loveliest youth that the eye could behold"—with Henry IV—"a man of very bad morals, great vices, intolerable pride, and infinite ambition."[59] Hume was the more dangerous enemy of Whiggism, and Hallam's narrative of Richard's reign, when read after Hume's, is like a disputatious echo.

The Parliament of 1386 which set up the commission to supervise the administration of Richard and to impeach the earl of Suffolk is the first major issue of difference. To Hume, Suffolk was wholly innocent. "Nothing can prove more fully the innocence of Suffolk, than the frivolousness of the crimes which his enemies, in the present plenitude of their power, thought proper to object against him."[60] Hallam answers this directly, if defensively. "The charges against this minister, without being wholly frivolous, were not so weighty as the clamour of the commons might have led us to expect."[61]

The commission, to Hume, Carte, and Hallam, was based on precedents going back to the previous century. Hume does not question

the legality of the commission. "It was easy to foresee that the intentions of the party were to render it perpetual"; such commissions "had
always been attended with extreme confusion"; Richard signed the
commission "which violence had extorted from him."[62] These are the
strongest things Hume had to say. Carte was much fiercer. To him, the
commission "divested the king of all his authority, making him a mere
cypher, and put all the power of the government into the hands of six,
or a majority, of the commission, who were most of them, as well as the
new Chancellor and Treasurer, the partisans or creatures of the duke of
Gloucester."[63] But to Hallam the commission is of great importance
and credit. He is at pains to refer to the high honor of the members of
the commission. There had been frequent instances of broken promises,
maladministration, and misappropriation of subsidies on the part of the
king. "No voice of his people," Hallam eloquently declaimed, "until it
spoke in thunder, would stop an intoxicated boy in the wasteful career
of dissipation." Strong remedies were required to preserve the still
unstable liberties of England. The constitution was possibly altered.
The royal prerogative was probably infringed. But "there is something
more sacred than the prerogative, or even than the constitution: the
public weal, for which all powers are granted and to which they must all
be referred. For this public weal it is to be confessed to be sometimes
necessary to shake the possessor of the throne out of his seat."

This doctrine rather damages the validity of Hallam's political
treatment of the past. For clearly he is conceding that legality may be
irrelevant to the principle of the "public weal." And who is to determine what is the public good? Legality, as Hallam demonstrated for
periods before the fourteenth century, was interpreted by lawyers. But
here, when the lawyers who reported to Richard at Nottingham on
whether the commission was legal, came down manifestly on the side of
the royal prerogative, Hallam says of their report, "perhaps extorted by
menaces . . . [it was] for the most part servile and unconstitutional."
The unhappiness of Hallam's arguments is displayed further when he
writes of the Merciless Parliament of 1388. "I shall pass slightly over
that season of turbulence, which afforded no legitimate precedent to
our constitutional annals." Hume and Carte both attributed the excesses to the factious conduct of the duke of Gloucester. Hallam half
agreed. Even so, he is keen to preserve some shreds of the honor of the
men who acted like the Long Parliament. "In every age," Hallam
pontificates, "it is the sophism of malignant and peevish men to traduce

the cause of freedom itself, on account of the interested motives by which its ostensible advocates have frequently been actuated."[64]

The eight years of royal rule that followed the king's coup d'état of 1389, proved to Hallam that, despite the importance of parliamentary commissions, the constitution was still so fragile that it was possible for the king to resume with ease the full prerogatives of the crown and to extend them illegally. The seizure of Thomas Haxey, a blunt member of Parliament, was "an open defiance of parliament and a declaration of absolute power." Excess followed excess. The Parliament of 1397 prosecuted those who had been prominent in the commission of 1387 and the Parliament of 1388. "In the fervour of prosecution this parliament could hardly go beyond that whose acts they were annulling; and each is alike unworthy to be remembered in the way of precedent." And yet, again, Hallam seeks to find, in spite of this "impartiality," a justification for the opponents of royal power. The leaders of the earlier parliaments, "though vindictive and turbulent, had a concern for the public interest; and after punishing their enemies, left the government upon its right foundation. In this [the Parliament of 1397], all regard for liberty was extinct."[65] David Hume had argued that "both parties, in their successive triumphs, seem to have had no further concern than that of retaliating on their adversaries; and neither of them were aware, that, by imitating they indirectly justified, as far as it lay in their power, all the illegal violence of the opposite party." Indeed, the later Parliament was perhaps more justified. There was a danger, wrote Hume, that "might have ensued from too much limitation" of a discretionary prerogative in time of perpetual disorders, turbulence, factions, and civil wars.[66]

In his summary of the revolution of 1399, Hallam takes issue with Hume and gives 1399 a special significance as the forerunner of 1688. The parallel of the two reigns goes so far that Hallam castigates Carte quite irrationally for taking Mowbray's side in his quarrel with Bolingbroke. Carte "viewed the whole of this reign and of those that ensued, with the jaundiced eye of Jacobitism."[67] Carte's remarks on Hereford being the instigator of this quarrel are little stronger than Hume's. Hume, whatever his Tory errors, was not suspected of being a Jacobite. Carte was.

In the history of historiography Hallam's treatment of the reign of Richard illustrates his importance as both a constitutional historian and as a medievalist. To the antiquarians in the century after Coke the medieval period was of contemporary relevance. The deposition of Richard II had been a precedent for that of James II. But the combination of Locke's political philosophy and the eighteenth century's sophisticated disdain for the barbaric Middle Ages made such an approach out of date, if not tasteless. Hume's account of the rival factions struggling for power was not written as "the Tory answer to Rapin"[68] nor yet to prove "the superiority of Tories to Whigs."[69] It is true that Hume derives an anti-Whig message from the factious reign of Richard: but a greater message is the irrelevance of comparing the fourteenth and seventeenth centuries.

Hallam, on the other hand, restored the significance of the Middle Ages to interpretations of the English constitution. It is not an imaginative reconstruction of medieval politics, nor a reading back of the nineteenth century into the Middle Ages. Hallam accepts many of the philosophical historians' attitudes to the barbarism of medieval times. His reading of the importance of the medieval English constitution combines the seventeenth- and eighteenth-century traditions. His arguments about the constitution are frequently about legality but, when legality fails, a securer basis of argument is utility. It is a Lockeian argument in terms of liberty, of public interest, and of the public weal. By using this terminology, Hallam retains fragments of the old seventeenth-century Cokeian interpretation. There is in Hallam's work an echo of Montesquieu and De Lolme. Both these continental lawyers saw the English constitution as a thing suspended in time. Hallam, however, wrote as an historian and documented his case conscientiously. His interpretation was to be retained throughout the nineteenth century. Stubbs, with only a slightly different approach, reaches much the same conclusions about the reign of Richard, but without the suggestions of contemporary relevance.

The Constitution in the Fifteenth Century

During the reigns of the Plantagenets, the constitution, in Hallam's opinion, was established in its fundamental points. "The whole fabric of English liberty rose step by step, through much toil, and many sacrifices: each generation adding some new security to the work, and trusting that posterity would perfect the labour as well as enjoy the reward." Hallam suggests that there were not "any essential privileges of our countrymen, any fundamental securities against arbitrary power, so far as they depend on positive institution, which may not be traced to the time when the house of Plantagenet filled the English throne."[70]

The essential character of this fifteenth-century constitution was a "monarchy greatly limited by law, though retaining much power that was ill calculated to promote the public good." In spite of this *political* allusion to the public good, Hallam at once states that it is not the place to discuss "what advantages might result from such a form of government": a disclaimer that weakens the invocation of "public good." It might be objected further that, as Hume argued, it was in the public interest for the crown to possess a residue of arbitrary power in the later Middle Ages. The constitution was not republican in the fifteenth century, Hallam says. Appeals, supplications, and petitions were always presented in humble language that exalted royal power. This, Hallam says, deceived such men as David Hume who thought erroneously that "all limitations of royal power during the fourteenth and fifteenth centuries were as much unsettled in law and in public opinion, as they were liable to be violated by force."[71] The contemporary records of Fortescue and Commines are appealed to as evidence of belief in limitations on the royal power.

Parliament, too, attained great power. The right to levy taxation was fixed: Edward II was the last king to tax without parliamentary consent. Parliament had gained the right to direct and check public expenditure. Parliament's supply depended on the redress of its grievances. Parliament secured the inviolability of its own statutes. By the Parliament of 1407 the right of controlling the administration by provisions was secured: "these provisions were by themselves hardly perhaps superior to the petition of right under Charles I."[72] Parliament had a right to impeach ministers. It also had its own privileges.

The Whig Interpretation

Parliament is stressed. In this Hallam's work represents a bridge over several centuries of historical development in Britain. Hallam is making use of those precedents that had been used by the Puritan opposition to Elizabeth in the sixteenth century; by Cokeian lawyers in the seventeenth century; and by antiquarians in the eighteenth century. And yet there are difficulties. His attitude to the value of a precedent is not the same. A precedent for Hallam was not a declaration absolute and universal. Indeed, as Hume pointed out, precedents were varied and offer no clear guidance if reliance is placed solely on them. There were for Hallam precedents like the judicial role of the Parliament of 1388 which "stands as a dangerous rock to be avoided, not a lighthouse to guide us along the channel."[73] (The present tense is significant. So is the immediacy of "us": eloquent encapsulations of the Cokeian tradition.) The precedents on which Hallam relied were rather the first instances of the constitution of Hallam's day.

Hallam's historical approach also looks forward to the Stubbsian idea of institutional development. Hallam is, in fact, tracing the emergence of the constitution of his day: hence, as with Stubbs, the overwhelming importance of Parliament and of the parliamentary control of the government. Hallam may well have misunderstood the nature and definition of Parliament in the *Middle Ages*. He probably overrated its powers. And he is certainly guilty of that "Whiggism" arraigned by Professor Butterfield in *The Whig Interpretation of History*—the ex post facto justification.

Like David Hume, Hallam was aware of the existence of many conflicting precedents in the past. But, unlike Hume, Hallam sees a *development* of the constitution. The arrangement of the post-1688 constitution is good. Only those precedents that anticipate the modern constitution are to be accepted. Hence his discrimination of precedents that correspond to the public good. This invocation of the public good as the ultimate authority in judging events in the fourteenth and fifteenth centuries is equivalent to the reliance Stubbs places on "the nation" at critical junctures in his *Constitutional History*.

In his work, Hallam used no unprinted sources, no public records. He used the same material that his predecessors for a century had used. Prynne, Madox, Hearne, and Rymer were the authorities he cited. Constitutional history was not to change much with the new methods that were used during the century. There was a greater skepticism perhaps, a keener argument about particular parliaments and undecided issues, but the approach was the same. "Was this or that event a stage in the development of parliamentary institutions?"—this is a question that Hallam, Stubbs, and Maitland would all have felt was important. Hume was less interested in this kind of question. Hume was a revolutionary historian insofar as his keenly analytical mind dissolved the issues of the past into fragments, explained them in an historical context and so exploded their significance as precedents. In this he followed in the wake of Spelman and Brady. To Hallam, the selection of precedents was part of his philosophical approach. In a famous passage, Hallam expostulated: "God forbid that our right to a just and free government should be tried by a jury of antiquaries!"[74] Here is his philosophical scorn for fact gathering. Philosophy meant, not an amassing of knowledge, but a judicious selection and interpretation of the evidence. Hence, also, his scorn for the lawyers' narrow approach of treating precedents as sacrosanct. The principle of Hallam's nonlegal approach and of his selection of the evidence is the development of a parliamentary system of government. Hallam accepted the evidence of Brady that Parliament, as it was later understood, did not exist before 1265. His history only becomes detailed when there is evidence to discuss. Parliamentary records only existed from the thirteenth century.

How did Hallam see his own function as an historian of medieval institutions? In a few pages he summarizes the attitudes to ancient liberties in the preceding century or so. "Mr. Hume's historical theory as to our constitution" has gradually made progress since its publication. "The tide of opinion, which since the Revolution, and indeed since the reign of James I, had been flowing so strongly in favour of the antiquity of our liberties, now seems, among the higher and more literary classes, to set pretty decidedly the other way." Hallam charges Hume with arguing that acts of force and injustice represent fair samples of the law and its administration. "We are deceived by the comparatively perfect state of our present liberties, . . . and are willing to be persuaded, that the whole scheme of English policy, . . . was at best but a mockery of popular privileges, hardly recognised in theory, and never regarded in effect." The argument against Brady, Carte, and Hume is simply that in the later Middle Ages, there was an awareness of the value of liberal institutions and of the fact that the king's powers were limited by "law." The very existence of this awareness, even though the idea did not triumph all the time, is enough to refute the "Tory" reading that the king was all-powerful. One might even be wrong as to what "law" was—as were Richard II's lawyers at Nottingham. But Hallam saw "law" as the idea of limited monarchy and as the peaceful development to the "comparatively perfect state of our present liberties."[75]

Hallam concluded his chapter with the complacent reflection on the improvement of the constitution and the establishment, in theory, of all the "essential privileges of our countrymen."[76] This sets the mood for the constitutional history for the next two centuries—how the Tudor monarchs assaulted the rights of Englishmen and how gradually under the Stuarts, English liberty and constitutionalism were asserted and finally triumphed with the Glorious Revolution of 1688.

Chapter Three
Constitutional History

Background to *Constitutional History*

Henry Hallam's *Constitutional History,* published in 1827, has been seen as the Whig answer to David Hume's *History* of seventy years earlier.[1] His intelligence, wit, style, and industry had made Hume's work a standard authority for a century. In the later editions, Hume made revisions, but these tended to strengthen the "Tory" bias of the work.[2] Although Hallam's work was indeed regarded as a reassuring Whig antidote to Hume, one is in danger of overlooking the importance of Hallam's approach, the novelty of which was demonstrated by the very title. Hallam is the first to use the two words together, thereby suggesting that there were other kinds of history than constitutional history, and that the constitution had an historical development. This approach had been suggested in 1787 with John Millar's *An Historical View of the English Government,* but this work had no great success in the first half of the nineteenth century.[3] Hallam's work is an attempt to trace the essential features of the English constitution, and he does this in a more historical context than two other influential writers who resemble Hallam in approach, J. L. de Lolme and A. V. Dicey.

Hume's *History* had been written backwards. That is to say, his first published volumes were on the seventeenth century. The next two volumes were on Tudor England; and finally, he dealt with the period before 1485. The comparative political stability of the eighteenth century depended, historically, on the resolution of the crises of the seventeenth century. Republicanism and Cromwell were denounced by Whig and Tory alike.[4] Even those who upheld the unfettered royal prerogative would hardly have rejoiced if George II or George III assumed the powers of Charles I's Council in the decade before 1640. The growth and extent of parliamentary rights, culminating in the Glorious Revolution, were of wide interest. Hume, though he accepted the Revolution, impugned the honor of the revolutionaries and launched a strong attack on Whiggish accounts of the iniquities of Charles I.

During the second half of the eighteenth century, Whig history was on the defensive.[5] Sir John Dalrymple, though himself a Whig, disclosed in his *Memoirs of Great Britain and Ireland* (1771) that, according to the French archives, Russell and other Whig heroes of 1688 had been simultaneously intriguing with France and that even Algernon Sidney had been in receipt of money from Barillon, the French ambassador. James Macpherson in 1775 published *Original Papers containing the Secret History of Great Britain from the Restoration till the Accession of George I.* In this, evidence was authoritatively displayed to show that, during the reign of William III, leading English politicians were also corresponding with the exiled James II.

There were, during this period, attempts to defend and, if possible, honor the parliamentary and Whig heroes. Mrs. Catherine Macaulay, Horace Walpole's "Dame Thucydides," published an eight-volume *History of England* between 1763 and 1783. Although she claimed to be "no bloody-minded Republican," her history was a strong indictment of Hume's from an advanced Whig standpoint. Hampden was her hero and her strongest invective was reserved for Oliver Cromwell, betrayer of the revolution. John Millar's *Historical View of the English Government,* dedicated to Charles James Fox, was a Scottish Whig answer to Hume: the work suggested an idea of progress implicit in the constitution. Thomas Somerville, another Scot, wrote a history of the late seventeenth century from a Whig point of view. Charles James Fox himself left a fragment of polemical history on the reign of James II.

But with the French Revolution and the war years, discussion of the rights and wrongs of monarchy in an historical context was seen in a new and alarming perspective. The death of Louis XVI in January 1793 had too much in common with the death of Charles I in 1649. In his *Sketch of Democracy* (1796) Robert Bisset attacked the Greek democracy as if it had been a popularly elected parliament and was as violent to Jack Cade as he would have been to Tom Paine.

After the war it was less difficult to keep the events of the recent past out of the seventeenth century. Even so, the radical Thomas Hinton Burley Oldfield published the still valuable six-volume *Representative History of Great Britain and Ireland* in 1816. His argument, implicit in the title, was mostly in the prefaces. In 1822 George Brodie published what he intended to be a counterblast to Hume—*History of the British Empire from the Accession of Charles I to the Restoration*. In this, drawing on unpublished material from a variety of sources, he attacked the Stuarts bitterly. A third major work, written from an anti-Hume point of view, was by the veteran radical, William Godwin. His *History of the Commonwealth* also dealt with the central years of the seventeenth century, and made use of the Thomasson tracts. It was only partly published when Hallam's work was being written.

In the 1820s there was a slight revival of interest in the Reformation century and a number of historians with a substantial readership wrote on the period. Robert Southey in *The Book of the Church* (1824) wrote a shrill defense of the Church of England. In this book he described at some length the persecutions and settlements of the sixteenth century. This prompted a reply from the Roman Catholic Charles Butler, who wrote a *Book of the Roman Catholic Church*. Another widely read work written from a sort of anti-Protestant bias was William Cobbett's *History of the "Reformation"* (1824–26). Hallam was implicily to attack Cobbett's view of the causal connection between the dissolution of the monasteries and the Elizabethan Poor Law. These were popular works that supplemented the general histories and had more appeal than the annalistic and martyrological works of John Strype and John Foxe.

By 1827 the two major reviews—the *Edinburgh Review* and the *Quarterly Review*—were teaching people history, the former from a Whig angle, the latter with a Tory bias. Articles, in the form of reviews of books, were a new genre of historical writing: a history in capsule. They were trailers for the multivolume works and were read far more widely than the works reviewed. In 1825 the young Macaulay published his first essay in the *Edinburgh Review*. It was an essay on Milton. The essay was not only about literature, but was also a vigorous and unequivocal defense of the revolution of the 1640s. Macaulay took issue with those—like Hume—who accepted 1688 but not 1641. "Let those who applaud the Revolution of 1688 and condemn the Rebellion, mention one act of James the Second to which a parallel is not to be found in the history of his father."[6] While refraining from approval of the execution of Charles, Macaulay defends the Long Parliament in their case against the king with the same vigor he displayed in defending the Reform Bill a few years later. This essay is one of the best-known works of historical writing of the 1820s. The impact it made should be remembered. In defending the Rebellion, Macaulay was defying the conservative analogy of the 1640s and the 1790s. By applauding the Parliamentarians, Macaulay was implicitly applauding Reform. His skill and power and style in such an organ as the *Edinburgh Review* made an impact denied to other writers with a similar aim, such as Godwin, Oldfield, or even Mrs. Macaulay.

Such was the historiographical background in 1827 when Hallam launched his *Constitutional History* on the world. The work opens with a brief statement of the nature of English government. "The government of England, in all times recorded by history, has been one of those mixed monarchies which the Celtic or Gothic appear universally to have established in preference to the coarse despotism of eastern nations, or to the more artificial tyranny of Rome and Constantinople, or to the various models of republican policy which were tried on the coasts of the Mediterranean Sea." The limits of the monarchy were established in 1485. For Hallam, the period of Tudor monarchy is a story of repeated encroachments on these constitutional limits. The Tudors succeeded "not certainly to be an absolute, but a vigorous prerogative."[7] Parliament and, in particular, the Commons had declined in their legitimate authority since the days of Edward III and Richard II.

The Early Tudors and the Constitution

The first two chapters of the work deal with the reigns of Henry VII, Henry VIII, Edward VI, and Mary I. Hallam divides the subject into political events and into ecclesiastical events. This causes some confusion, but one can see a possible historiographical explanation. In the first chapter, Hallam is dealing with what he regarded as erroneous political interpretations of the constitution, above all those of David Hume. In the second, the enemies are the ecclesiastical historians, both High Churchmen such as Collier and Roman Catholics such as his contemporaries, Charles Butler and John Lingard.

The constitutional issue that was an historiographical issue was the role of Parliament during these reigns. David Hume was keen throughout his volumes on Tudor England to minimize the role of Parliament. The Parliament of 1485 was "obsequious." "In vain did the people look for protection from the parliament, which was frequently summoned during the reign [of Henry VII]." Henry VIII summoned a convocation and a parliament in 1523: "and found neither of them in a disposition to complain of the infringement of their privileges: it was only doubted how far they would carry their liberality to the King." The English "had reason to dread each meeting of that assembly and were then sure of having tyranny converted into law." When in 1539 they gave the king's proclamations the power of statute, "without scruple or deliberation they made by one act a total subversion of the English constitution." The Parliament of 1546 is condemned for being "servile and prostitute." "It was the usual maxim [of Parliament] to acquiesce in every administration which was established." The letters to sheriffs recommending the election of particular men sent in 1552 were "an expedient which could not have been practised, or even imagined, in an age where there was any idea or comprehension of liberty."[8]

Hallam is ready to concede that Parliament acted feebly; but at the same time he deduces the maxim of the supremacy of Parliament, legally if not effectually. Of the statute of 1539, Hallam thought that, far from it being "an instance of servile compliance," it was "a striking testimony to the free constitution it infringed, and demonstrates that the prerogative could not soar to the heights it aimed at, till thus imped [i.e., grafted] by the perfidious hand of parliament." And although Henry VIII was indeed able to dominate his parliaments in general, yet he met with opposition in 1532 when "so unquestionable were the legislative rights of parliament, [that] . . . although much displeased, even Henry was forced to yield." Parliament's importance, further-more, is demonstrated by "the anxiety of the court to obtain favourable elections."[9] In other words, illegal actions and abuses imply the existence, even though in theory, of laws and of correct usage in constitutional matters. Hallam's desire to redeem the credit of Tudor parliaments from Hume's scorn seems not to meet Hume's arguments at their weakest points. Hume allows that the early Tudor parliaments conceded England's "ancient privileges" and subverted the "English constitution." But what, for Hume, were these ancient privileges? What was the "constitution"? Hume, in his empirical treatment of history, has always been loath to admit the validity of such concepts. To Hallam the concession and subversion are vindications of the existence of privileges and a constitution that was above all the individuals of the past. Hume and Hallam agree, it would appear, on the facts. Their disagreement turns on interpreting the historical significance of Parliament.

What, Hallam wondered, had happened to "that English spirit which had not only controlled such injudicious princes as John and Richard II, but withstood the first and third Edward in the fulness of their pride and glory?" The "people" were not acquiescent. Periodic rebellion and the "independent spirit" of the commons bear witness to that. But what was deplorable was the compliance of the aristocracy to the sanguinary demands of Henry VIII's imperious will. "Nor was this selfish and pusillanimous subserviency more characteristic of the minions of Henry's favour, the Cromwells, the Riches, the Pagets, the Russells, and the Powletts, than on the representatives of ancient and honourable houses, the Norfolks, the Arundels, and the Shrewsburies."[10]

The English Reformation

John Lingard's volume of his *History of England* dealing with the Reformation had appeared in 1820. This particular volume had been praised by the *Edinburgh Review* and approved by the Vatican. It was condemned by the English Ultramontane bishop, Joseph Milner, but Hallam was the first to criticize Lingard from a middle-of-the-road Protestant Whig point of view. Hallam's views on the Reformation and Roman Catholicism and his general appreciation of Lingard are discussed elsewhere. At times in the *Constitutional History,* Hallam tends to discount Lingard's views on the Tudor period, because of his Roman Catholicism. Lingard's "acuteness and industry would raise him to a very respectable place among our historians, if he could have repressed the inveterate partiality of his profession." Lingard is arraigned for softening his account of Mary Tudor: "A man of sense should be ashamed of such a miserable partiality to his sect." Lingard's authorities are impugned: "his readers probably do not esteem [Father Persons] quite as much as he does. If he had attended to Burnet, he would have a more sufficient voucher." The nonjuror, Jeremy Collier, who wrote *An Ecclesiastical History of Great Britain* partly as an answer to Burnet's *History of the Reformation,* is treated in like manner. Collier's High Church views are scorned. "We should be on our guard against the

Romanizing high-church men, such as Collier, and the whole class of antiquaries, Wood, Hearne, Drake, Browne Willis, & c, who are, with hardly an exception, partial to the monastic orders, and sometimes scarcely keep on the mask of protestantism." In Collier's view of things, "it had been better to give up the Reformation entirely, than to suffer one reflection on the clergy." Elsewhere Collier "descants, in the true spirit of a high churchman, on the importance of confession."[11] With all these declarations of disagreement, Hallam rarely comes to issue with Lingard and Collier. In such a work as the *Constitutional History* this is possibly not to be expected. His differences with his predecessors emerge in the general account of the English Reformation which, in spite of the partisan remarks already quoted, follows Hume in being free, generally speaking, from any particular ecclesiastical party feeling.

According to Hallam, the English Reformation was well prepared. Wycliffe and the Lollards had taught nearly the same doctrines as Luther. A difference is drawn between the pope's spiritual authority upheld by the Gallicans and his jurisdictional authority. The former "dropped off as a dead branch, when the axe had lopped the fibres that gave it nourishment."[12] The loppings were the legislation of the Parliament of 1529, the dissolution of the monasteries, and the new liturgy. In these attitudes Hallam and Hume are close together.

Hallam considers the dissolution of the monasteries in some detail. He is at pains to defend Cromwell's visitations. "The reports of these visitors were so minute and specific, that it is rather a preposterous degree of incredulity to ignore them, whenever it bears hard on the regulars." The fact that some monastic houses were commended for their unexceptionable purity "may afford a presumption that the censure of others was not an indiscriminate prejudging of their merits." (This is an argument similar to his assertion of evidence for constitutional liberty under the Tudors.) The rights of corporate property were not to be treated in the same way as private personal property. Public policy outweighed these rights. The dispossessed monks were not ill treated. "Compare [their pensions] with those generally and justly thought munificent, which this country bestows on her veterans of Chelsea and Greenwich." Hallam criticizes those who, like Cobbett, had argued that "the alms of monasteries maintained the indigent throughout the kingdom, and that the system of parochial relief, so much the topic of complaint, was rendered necessary by the dissolution of those beneficent foundations. . . . But the blind eleemosynary spirit inculcated by the Romish church is notoriously the cause, not the cure, of beggary and wretchedness." The successors of the abbots were renowned for their charity and munificence. "And better it had been that these revenues should thus from age to age have been expended in liberal hospitality, in discerning charity, in the promotion of industry and cultivation, in the active duties or even generous amusements of life, than in maintaining a host of ignorant and inactive monks, in deceiving the population by a superstitious pageantry, in the encouragement of idleness and mendicity."[13]

Hallam does, however, have criticisms of the dissolutions. The nature of these criticisms suggests that Hallam sees himself not so much as a philosophical historian seeking causes and the inner core of truth, but rather as a constitutional and political adviser. This is a role that Hallam takes on more and more as he moves toward his own times. The dissolution was rushed. "A few years would not [have been] ill consumed in contriving new methods of attaining the beneficial effects which monastic institutions had not failed to produce, and in preparing the people's minds for so important an innovation."[14] Instead of turning the monks adrift, it would have been better to forbid men to take vows and to let monasteries die out slowly—an idea which seems to owe more to Pitt's abolition of sinecures than to the realities of the sixteenth century.

After political comment, Hallam reverts to discussion of the social consequences of the dissolution. The acquisition of the monastic property by the new class of courtiers and gentry led to a stabilization of the Reformation. The members of Parliament, even in Mary's reign, so obsequious in all matters of religion, adhered with a firm grasp to the possession of church lands. "Not that these gentlemen were hypocritical pretenders to a belief they did not entertain, but that according to the general laws of human nature, they gave a readier acceptance to truths which made their estates more secure." There was a consequence also, "of no slight advantage to our civil constitution, strengthening and as it were infusing new blood into the territorial aristocracy, who were to withstand the enormous prerogative of the crown."[15]

Political advice comes back again in the discussion of the reign of Edward VI. Hallam's cautious Whiggish temperament made him feel that the speedy Protestant legislation of that reign provoked the insurrection of 1549. German troops, according to Burnet, were used to quell the seditious spirit in the nation. "It might be asked," Hallam writes, as if he is remonstrating against radical legislation of his own day,

whether in the acknowledged coexistence of two religions, some preference were not fairly claimed for the creed which all had once held, and which the greater part yet retained: whether it were becoming that the counsellors of an infant king should use such violence in breaking up the ecclesiastical constitution; whether it were to be expected that a free-spirited people should see their conscience thus transferred by proclamation, and all that they had learned to venerate not only torn away from them, but exposed to what they must reckon blasphemous contumely and profanation.[16]

The moral for statesmen is not to provoke the people to revolt. Such passages angered robust Protestants such as Southey. Yet the political lesson is the same as that put forward by David Hume when that historian discussed the Pilgrimage of Grace. The constitution is laid bare by the bold statement that "there are certain bounds beyond which the most slavish submission cannot be extended." From this political adage Hume switches back to historical analysis. "All the late innovations, particularly the dissolution of the smaller monasteries, and the imminent danger to which all the rest were exposed, had bred discontent among the people, and had disposed them to revolt."[17] Such passages show how similar in spirit and treatment Hallam and Hume were. Disputes between them seem to be reduced to trifles. Yet these trifles were of great emotional significance and led to politically fundamental questions such as, where does power lie? Where should it lie? Was this person justified in acting in such a way? On what grounds does one determine the justification? On grounds of "legality"? Or of public policy? Or should one, in looking at the past, disregard such notions? Problems like these became critical again in the reign of Elizabeth.

The Reign of Elizabeth

It was partly the object of Hallam's chapter on Elizabethan government "to correct [Hume's] exaggerated outline; and nothing would be more easy than to point at other mistakes into which he has fallen

through prejudice, through carelessness, or through want of acquaintance with law."[18] Hallam had rated Hume for his careless approach to
law in the *Middle Ages*.[19] David Hume had angered Whigs by his
remark that "the government of England during that age, however
different in other particulars, bore, in this respect, some resemblance to
that of Turkey at present." During the eighteenth and nineteenth
centuries, the Turkish government was seen as the last word in tyranny,
and Burke in the 1790s justified even a policy of revolution there.
Hume had probably derived the Turkey analogy from Raleigh's *History
of the World* in which Philip II of Spain is said to have aimed at absolute
monarchy "over the Netherlands like unto the Kings and sovereigns of
England and France" and, "Turklike, to trample on all privileges and
fundamental rights":[20] a passage quoted by Hume as illustrating
contemporary public opinion on the English monarchy.

Hume distinguished two approaches to constitutional history: first,
one must ask of a particular circumstance, "What was best?" and, in
discussing the constitution, "What was established?" In an appendix to
the chapters on Elizabethan history Hume discusses the latter question.
The monarchy was unquestionably absolute. He gives instances of
arbitrary justice after one of which he goads insular Whig readers with
the remark that "it would be difficult to produce an instance of such an
act of authority in any place nearer than Muscovy." Men were impris-
oned without trial; pressment was rife. Loans, ship money, and benevo-
lences were enforced. The legislative power of Parliament was ineffec-
tive in the face of the queen's dispensing power and of the force of her
proclamations. Those proclamations about dress resembled "the
method employed by the great Czar Peter." Parliament, furthermore,
was of no use in the defense of liberty. "The persecuting statutes which
they passed against papists and puritans are extremely contrary to the
genius of freedom." "It was only during the next generation [after the
1580s] that the noble principles of liberty took root; and, spreading
themselves under the shelter of puritannical absurdities, became fashionable among the people." Shakespeare is invoked as a contemporary
who makes "scarcely any mention of civil liberty, which some pretended historians have imagined to be the object of all the ancient
quarrels, insurrections and civil wars." The real check on this royal
power was custom and the physical limits imposed by what the people
would tolerate. "As the prince commanded no mercenary army, there

was a tacit check on him, which maintained the government in that medium to which the people had been accustomed."[21]

Hallam, too, divides his treatment of the reign of Elizabeth. Two chapters deal with the laws relating to Catholics and to Puritans: to what Hume would have called the problem of "What is best?" The third chapter deals with the government, dealing with what was established. Hallam concedes that the queen and her government acted in an absolute way. She was jealous of her prerogatives, especially those relating to ecclesiastical affairs. Hallam is particularly severe on the Elizabethan penal legislation and deprecates attempts to diminish its efficiency or extent. He lists stages of religious persecution. "The statutes of Elizabeth's reign comprehend every one of those progressive degrees of restraint and persecution." These measures were prompted not only by bigotry, but also by an arbitrary spirit of government. Burleigh, moreover, interfered in all sorts of private matters so that England seemed "as if it had been the household estate of a nobleman under a strict and prying steward." Some of the arbitrary excesses may be excused. Proclamations, which were of indefinite authority, nonetheless supplemented legislation. Now, "since the English constitution has reached its zenith," a statute deals with every possible mischief and the swollen statute book has "at least put an end to such exertions of prerogative." The Court of the Star Chamber, though illegal, was "so well established as to pass without any murmurs."[22]

Yet parliament was "not quite so servile and submissive as an artful historian has represented it."[23] Knollys, Hatton, and Cecil sought seats in the Commons. The crown was keen to influence elections. The number and prestige of members of Parliament increased. All this was a recognition of the significance of Parliament and of the House of Commons. Parliament's growing legal authority was also indicated by the establishment during Elizabeth's reign of its leading privileges.

The processes of law were preserved. Hallam asserts that there had been no power of arbitrary imprisonment since 1215. "The writ of habeas corpus has always been a matter of right." Discretionary imprisonment by the privy council was illegal. The existence of this remained, however much they were abused, and "imposed a degree of seeming restraint on the crown, and wounded that pride which is commonly a yet stronger sentiment than the lust of power." Hallam agrees—not very convincingly—that "it was rather the weakness than the vigour of her government which led to its inquisitorial watchfulness and harsh measures of prevention."[24] So whereas Hume and Hallam would agree that the later Tudor monarchy was strong and powerful, Hume argued that it was limited by custom and the facts of power; Hallam that it was limited by existing forms and processes of law, which themselves enshrined ancient principles of constitutional liberty.

What about the evidence of contemporary opinions? Hallam treats Hume's invocation of Raleigh with scant respect. "Who, that is really desirous of establishing the truth, would have brought Raleigh into court as an unexceptionable witness on such a question? Unscrupulous ambition taught men in that age who sought to win the crown's favour, to falsify all law and fact in behalf of prerogative, as unblushingly as our modern demagogues exaggerate and distort the liberties of the people." In turn Hallam calls forth his own contemporary witness. Christopher Yelverton's speech in 1571 claiming that the prince's prerogatives were limited was "the true voice of English liberty." Aylmer, afterward bishop of London, wrote a pamphlet against John Knox, in which he defended regiments of women. In this he argued that "it is not in England so dangerous a matter to have a woman ruler, as men take it to be. For first, it is not she that ruleth, but the laws, the executors whereof be her judges appointed by her, her justices and such other officers. Secondly, she maketh no statutes or laws, but the honourable court of parliament." Hallam's principal contemporary witness is Richard Hooker. Hooker, who mingled among ecclesiastical controversialists "like a knight of romance among caitiff brawlers," resembles Locke in his explicit derivation of the origin of government from a primary contract. He saw society existing under law. Hallam goes so far as to say that "his Whig principles, in the last book, are announced with a temerity that would have startled his superiors." Even so, Hallam recognized that contemporary writers contradicted each other; this did not invalidate either, however. The upholders of absolute monarchy like Sir Thomas Smith and Sir Walter Raleigh, argues Hallam, insinuate their tenets "by means of vague and obscure generalities." Those who maintain a limited monarchy and popular rights, on the other hand, "use a distinct and intelligible language." But the mere declaration of these rights proves their existence; the violation of rights implies their existence. "The remonstrance of the judges against arbitrary imprisonment by the Council is infinitely more conclusive to prove that the right of personal liberty existed, than the fact of the infringement can to prove that it did not."[25] Heads I win, tails you lose.

Hallam concludes his chapter on the Tudors with a definition of the government as a "monarchy greatly limited by law, but retaining much power that was ill calculated to promote the public good, and swerving continually into an irregular course, which there was no restraint adequate to check."[26]

Precedents and Continuity

This then was Hallam's answer to Hume. Yet there are a number of historiographical problems that remain. What was a precedent? Hallam uses the word frequently. Do instances of arbitrary government make precedents? The jurisdiction of the Court of Star Chamber "had been so well established as to pass without many audible murmurs." Did this legitimize it? The House of Commons was far "from exercising powers which by ancient precedent they might have claimed as their own."[27] If a right, for which there is an ancient precedent, is forfeited, does this annul the precedent? This is the issue with government accountability to Parliament, which went by default under the Tudors. If a right is gained, does this make it fundamental, even though there is no medieval authority of the right? This is a problem arising from parliamentary privilege which becomes defined only under Elizabeth. Does one accept the later or the earlier precedent? In the face of so many precedents, the historian has to select his precedents. "Evidence" may be a more fitting word than "precedent" in the circumstances, for the latter has overtones of precision and legal obligation. As was shown in the chapter on the *Middle Ages,* Hallam was selective in his precedents. It emerges similarly in his treatment of Tudor government that he is only interested in those precedents that looked forward to his own day when the constitution was at its "zenith."

This suggests a further difficulty. Can one deal with the constitution in an historical way? Do not different components of the constitution have different meanings and values at different times? What is there in common between the medieval and the nineteenth-century Parliament beyond the name? Similarly, was the notion of "law" that Hooker had the same notion that Hallam had? Hooker's idea of "law" was the medieval concept far different from the Cokeian precision of common law.[28] Hallam's arguments are essentially Cokeian. The polemical power of Cokeian precedent was much weakened by the time of Hallam. Yet he was invoking the words of Hooker in a cause that postdates Hooker in language and argument. Hallam's attribution of Whig ideas to him displays this weakness. It is as unhelpful to an understanding of Hooker and his times as the statement that Aquinas was the first Whig is to an appreciation of Scholasticism.

But what is the value of Hallam's other contemporary witnesses: Christopher Yelverton and the Elizabethan Puritans? Hallam is harsh on the early Puritans, some of whose writings in asserting a separate and all-powerful church "call to mind those tones of infatuated arrogance which had been heard from the lips of Gregory VIII." They are shown to be outsiders in the Elizabethan system, unscrupulous zealots, a persecuted sect. Their ecclesiastical ideas, however, had political implications. "Their denial, indeed, of the queen's supremacy . . . might justly be considered as a derogation of her temporal sovereignty." Many members of Parliament displayed a tendency to Puritanism. In the reign of Elizabeth, the chief instances

of a high-strained prerogative . . . have some relation to ecclesiastical matters; and herein the temper of the predominant religion was such as to account no measures harsh or arbitrary that were adopted towards its conquered but still formidable enemy. Yet when the royal supremacy was to be maintained against a different foe by less violent acts of power, it revived the smouldering embers of English liberty. The stern and exasperated puritans became the depositories of that sacred fire.

This, oddly enough, resembles the words of Hume, already quoted, about the "puritannical absurdities" sheltering the noble principles of liberty. By making the Puritans the upholders of ideas of constitutional liberty, Hallam is suggesting a continuity with the medieval past which, on other evidence, does not exist. The Puritans, as Hallam says, derived their political ideas from their ecclesiastical ideas: from the Mosaic rather than the ancient law. This was not the inspiration for the opponents of John and Richard II. By invoking the Puritans as contemporary witnesses and then by examining their tenets, he is weakening his case that there was something permanent in the concepts of the constitution from the thirteenth to the seventeenth century; that the

Puritans of the reign of Elizabeth and, more particularly, her two successors, were "a race of men in whom the spirit of those who stood against John and Edward was rekindled with a less partial and a steadier warmth."[29]

Puritanism, Archbishop Laud, and the Constitution

The Puritan's foe in the reigns of Elizabeth's two successors was William Laud. The historiographical treatment of Laud has depended on far more than a historian's treatment of Puritanism. During the nineteenth century there were changing interpretations of Laud. As with the historiography of Becket, interest in the hapless prelate was stimulated by the Oxford movement. Southey's defense of Laud is largely a personal one and resembles Wordsworth's ecclesiastical sonnet on him. Laud's "love of learning," Southey wrote in *The Book of the Church,* "his liberal temper, his munificence, and his magnanimity, would have made him an honour and a blessing to the Church in its happiest ages; his ardent, incautious, sincere, uncompromising spirit, were ill adapted to that in which his lot had fallen."[30] This is an echo of Hume, who wrote that Laud chose to introduce new ceremonies when "the humor of the nation ran at that time in the extreme opposition to superstition."[31]

But from the 1840s there was a new partisan interest in Laud, which reached its peak with Mozley's remark that Laud "saved the English church."[32] Laud is seen by the High Churchmen not merely as a man who aimed to bring the Church of England away from Protestant sectarianism and into a Catholic community. The ritualists stressed his revival of ceremonies; Oxonians his patronage of learning. Laud was appreciated for his personal qualities, but not in the hagiographical manner of Southey, who writes little of Laud's life and much of his death. More than one High Church biography explicitly attacked the idea of the man put out by Hallam and Macaulay.[33] But the criticism of Hallam's view did not really meet what Hallam said. Hallam's cold criticism of the archbishop is based on four points. First, Laud was an innovator. "Whatever doubts may be raised as to the Calvinism of Cranmer and Ridley, there can surely be no room for any as to the chiefs of the Anglican church under Elizabeth." Second, he had a dash of popery. This, Hallam allows, depends on what one means by popery. It means "an acknowledgment of the supremacy, in faith and discipline, of the Roman see"; or "those tenets which were rejected as corruptions of Christianity at the Reformation"; or "the ceremonies and ecclesiastical observances which were set aside at the same time." In the last sense, Laud was guilty of inclining to Rome; his work was seen as an abandonment of the Protestant cause. The prominent conversions to Rome of people of high rank added to contemporary suspicions. This connivance with the converts together with the apparent reluctance to exact the full rigors of the penal laws against recusants may seem just and tolerant. "Unfortunately, the prosecution of the sectaries renders it difficult to ascribe such a liberal principle to the council of Charles I." The belief in the divine right of episcopacy—"a doctrine of which the first traces, as I apprehend, are found about the end of Elizabeth's reign"—was seen by Laud's party as indispensably requisite to a Christian church. Hence they treated the Presbyterians "with insolence abroad, and severity at home." Laud's intolerant persecution of the Puritan clergy was "not from bigotry, which in the moral sense he never displayed, but systematic policy." Laud advised "a declaration enjoining silence on the controverted points; a measure by no means unwise, if it had been fairly acted upon. It is alleged, however, that the preachers on one side only were silenced, the printers of books on one side censured in the Star-chamber, while full scope was indulged to the opposite sect." And the fourth charge was the most serious. Laud was Charles's principal minister. He had "placed before his eyes the aggrandizement, first of the Church, and next of the royal prerogative, as his end and aim in every direction." He not only took a prominent share in the severities of the Star Chamber, but as his correspondence shows, "perpetually lamented that he was restrained from going further lengths." Laud's letters to Strafford in Ireland reveal the yearnings for a more thorough policy. Laud and Strafford were kindred spirits in stretching the prerogative to the uttermost limits. "Do we think the administration of Charles during the interval of parliaments rash and violent? They tell us it was over-cautious and slow. Do we revolt from the severities of the Star-chamber? To Laud and Strafford they seemed the feebleness of excessive levity."[34]

Hallam's treatment of Laud is of an ecclesiastical politician. His reference to Laud's "sect" reveals much. Hallam does not consider whether Laud's beliefs were right or wrong; he is only interested in their effect on the constitution of England and on the lives of Englishmen.

The ritual, revival of fastings, restoration of churches are really private matters. But Laud's errors consist in the attempt to impose ceremonies on the whole church at the expense of the persecuted Puritans who conscientiously believed otherwise. The Puritans, in the 1640s, were equally wrong in ejecting those clergy who did not accept their view of things. Above all, Laud had incorrect views of the constitution and was, during the 1630s, the chief adviser to Charles, during the eleven years without parliaments.

Form and Essence and the Crisis of 1640–41

And how does one determine the "correct" view of the constitution at this time? Hallam does not measure the correctness solely by its fruits. He concedes that the 1630s were a period of prosperity but it "was the natural course of things that wealth should be progressive in such a land." The idea of an existing constitution, independent of both time and circumstance, has to be posited. Hallam's idea of legality and his approach to the tender issues of the reign of Charles I have vestiges of that seventeenth-century legalism derived from Coke. Yet his view of the constitution is also fitted into a kind of philosophical nominalism. Hallam sees a difference between the form and the essence of things. This was a distinction of which he was conscious from his early twenties, and in his major works one can see the working out of this distinction continually. Hallam assumes a knowledge of the common facts of history. It is assumed, for example, that his readers are familiar with Hume's work. And "every one of my readers is acquainted more or less with the theological tenets of original sin, free will and predestination." The circumstances of the death of Mary, Queen of Scots "are well known matters of history upon which it is unnecessary to dwell." The details of the Revolution of 1688 "are minutely known to almost all my readers."[35] Hallam would regard this common knowledge as the "form" of history; what he wished to find out was its "essence." In the same way, he wanted to get at the realities of the constitution and the legalities of actions. The structure of power is only the form; the essence of the constitution is unchanging and has been the same since the thirteenth century. To Hume's two questions that an historian must ask himself, Hallam adds a third: "What was the essence behind the form?" Yet Hallam is elusive when one seeks to pin down his idea of the essence: unless that essence comes nearest to coinciding with the form during the period of comparative stability from 1689 to 1827. In the seventeenth century there were precedents for various principles of the constitution, such as Parliament being the sole authority for the levying of taxation, but there were also the precedents for an unfettered royal prerogative. And if the lawyers were divided, what value does one place on the idea of legality? The difficulties of Hallam's position can be seen in his discussion of the Petition of Right, the administration of Charles I, and the constitutional settlements of the Long Parliament.

Judges rejected the plea for habeas corpus by the gentlemen committed for refusing to contribute toward a loan. The Petition of Right arose out of the consequent parliamentary concern for fundamental liberty and was a statement of constitutional rights in defiance of what were regarded as illegal exactions. What was at stake was the interpretation of liberty. Hallam sees the dilemma: who, but judges, interpret the law? If the judges say that parliamentary claims are ill-founded, to what other authority does one resort? Hallam gets over this difficulty in two ways. First, he defends the petitioners' rejection of the judgment by invoking politics rather than the law; and, second, he points out that the reasons the judges gave in declaring for the king avoided "the more extravagent tenets of absolute monarchy"—the victory thereby being with the petitioners. The consequences of the judges' decision were "that every statute from the time of Magna Carta, designed to protect the personal liberties of Englishmen, became a dead letter; since the insertion of four words in a warrant (per speciale mandatum regis), which might become matter of form, would control their remedial efficacy. And this wound was the more deadly, in that the notorious cause of the gentlemen's imprisonment was their withstanding an illegal exaction of money." The king assented to the Petition. This assent should have rendered superfluous those four words. "This latest and most complete recognition must sweep away all contrary precedent, and could not without a glaring violation of its obvious meaning be stretched into an admission of ship-money." The king, by raising extraparliamentary revenue after 1629, and, in particular, ship money, was thus manifestly behaving illegally. The judges' consent to these measures meant that the law was subordinated to the king. This, of course, is what Charles and his flattering courtiers wanted. Yet there is still a difference in outlook between the lawyers and the courtiers. Occasionally, there is a reluctance among the lawyers to go to all the lengths that the courtiers wished. In Felton's case, for example, when Charles expressed a desire that the assassin of the duke of Buckingham be tortured, the judges declared unanimously that "the law of England did not allow the use of torture. This is a remarkable proof that, amidst all the arbitrary principles and arbitrary measures of the time, a truer sense of the inviolability of the law had begun to prevail, and that the free constitution of England was working off the impurities with which violence had stained it." The crown lawyers were regarded by Laud and Strafford as falling behind the expectations of the court, "and their scruples were reckoned the chief shackles on the half emancipated prerogative." And, in the case of ship money, lawyers like Noy in preparing the levy made an acknowledgment of the ancient constitution by discovering dubious precedents from parchments in the Tower. And even Strafford himself, at the peak of unfettered prerogative, preserved vestiges of constitutionalism. He never wanted to abolish the use of parliaments, "whether from remains of attachment to ancient forms of liberty surviving amidst the hatred of the real essence, or from the knowledge that a well-governed parliament is the best engine for extracting money from the people."[36]

These recognitions of constitutionalism defy the arguments of Hume that precedents for particular points of power are uncertain and ambiguous. The recognition suggests that there was a legal constitution that was above the crown and the Parliament. At one place Hallam despairs of precedents for constitutionalism altogether. Precedents, he says, after discussing the history of the militia, are "apt to be much more records of power than of right." The argument with Charles then becomes political rather than legal. If the monarchy is regarded as absolute, if the royal prerogative is unbounded, then there can be no security whatsoever for life, liberty, or property. Charles acted as if this was the case, and gradually men became completely skeptical about his pledged word. The king accepted the Petition of Right, but levied the illegal ship money soon afterward. "The council of Charles the First, and the hirelings who ate his bread, . . . resorted rather to the favourite topic of the times, the intrinsic absolute authority of the king." The king himself aimed at ruling the country without parliaments, like "his brothers of France and Spain."[37]

It was a conflict of political approaches to the constitution that led to the crises of 1640 and 1641. When the Long Parliament was finally summoned in 1640, its members felt that new securities were needed for the preservation of liberties which, however venerable, had been assaulted. The Long Parliament in the first nine months of its existence "made scarce any material change in our constitution, such as it had been established and recognised under the Plantagenets." By getting rid of the Court of Star Chamber and the Court of Ecclesiastical Commission, "the balance of our constitution might seem rather to have been restored to its former equipoise, than to have undergone any fresh change." Parliament was to be summoned at fixed intervals and the machinery of the calling of Parliament to be placed beyond the power of the king to evade. By these provisions "the long parliament formed our constitution such nearly as it now exists. Laws of greater importance were doubtless enacted in subsequent times, particularly at the Revolution; but none of them perhaps were strictly necessary for the preservation of our civil and political privileges; and it is rather from 1641, than any other epoch, that we may date their full legal establishment."[38]

But the Long Parliament began to arrogate rights to itself and became as illegal and arbitrary as the king. The country went through the horrors of a civil war and, says Hallam cautiously in a tacit allusion to Macaulay's recent essay on Milton, "even when posterity may have cause to rejoice in the ultimate revolt, the existing generation are seldom compensated for their present loss of tranquility." What went wrong? Hallam argues that "the single false step which rendered his affairs irretrievable by any thing short of civil war, and placed all reconciliations at an insuperable distance, was Charles' attempt to seize the five members within the walls of the house, an evident violation, not of common privilege, but of all security for the independent existence of parliament in the mode of its execution."[39] This made uncertain even those extra securities that Parliament had introduced. It also resulted in an alienation between Parliament and Charles which led to the most striking encroachments of the royal prerogative by Parliament—the act that Parliament could be neither dissolved nor prorogued without its own consent, and the placing of the militia under parliamentary control.

Civil War and Interregnum

Hallam's long discussion as to whether "a thoroughly upright and enlightened man would rather have enlisted under the royal or parliamentary standard" is well-known. Neither side had a monopoly of right or wrong. He sees attractive spirits among the royalists, unconstitutional fanatics among the parliamentarians. Partisanship in war is a different problem from campaigning for parliamentary rights under an arrogant king. Excesses such as the deaths of Strafford, Laud, and Charles are viewed with ascending degrees of disapproval. With respect to Charles's death, "if it be alleged that many of the regicides were firmly persuaded in their consciences of the right and duty of condemning the King, we may surely remember that private murderers have often had the same apology."[40]

The period of the war and the Interregnum might, Hallam argues, not strictly belong "to a work which undertakes to relate the progress of the English constitution, but this would have left a sort of chasm that might disappoint the reader." To avoid this disappointment, and since "more general political history, without a knowledge of which the laws and government of any people must be unintelligible,"[41] Hallam devotes a long chapter to the period. In making these remarks Hallam reveals a dilemma of his approach to the work and to the English constitution. His work had two facets, not always happily yoked together. In the first place, as has been seen, it was a description of the eternal verities of the constitution: principles that had been declared in the reigns of the Plantagenets. In the second place it was a history of the development of the constitution from medieval origins to its zenith, as Hallam saw it, in 1827. These two facets may be reconciled by arguing that the history of the constitution was the progressive establishment of the declared Plantagenet values in the face of acts of aggression by the Tudor and Stuart monarchs. Yet the dilemma remains at critical periods and the Interregnum was one such. There was an interruption of progressive development. England, being ever a limited monarchy, was far from being "constitutional" or "legal" under the conditions imposed by Civil War and Cromwell. On the other hand, what was the relationship of the period 1642–60 to the generation before 1642 or to the years after 1660?

In the chapter on the Interregnum there is a revealing and, to Tories, highly provocative discussion of the claims of Cromwell to kingship. Hallam sees nothing outrageous in the claim. He considered possession of the crown as the principal justification for regarding its holder as king: and this on political as well as on legal grounds. "The right of excluding an unworthy heir from the succession," he writes later in discussing the Exclusion Bill crisis, "was supported not only by the plain and fundamental principles of civil society . . . but by those of the English constitution." This approach to legitimacy leads him to regard Cromwell's Protectorate after 1657 as "substantially a monarchy and [it] ought to be placed in that class, notwithstanding the unimportant difference in the style of the sovereign." (In later editions, "unimportant" is omitted.) The style of the Petition and Advice was that of subjects humbly addressing a monarch. The solemnities with which he was inaugurated were those applicable to monarchs. An oath of allegiance was taken "to the protector singly, without any mention of the commonwealth." Oliver could well have become king in name and have founded a house with distinction. "The English monarchy would have revived with less lustre in the eyes of the vulgar, but with more security for peace and freedom, in the line of Cromwell. Time would have worn away the stains of ignoble birth and criminal usurpation." This commonsense, empirical approach is one of Hallam's strengths. He is able to strip political problems of any dazzling mystique and, like Walter Bagehot, appreciate the realities of *power,* shorn of its trappings. "The science of politics," he says elsewhere, "like that of medicine, must content itself with devising remedies for immediate dangers." And he censures those historians who glide over Cromwell's administration as merely "an usurpation, which can furnish no precedent, and consequently does not merit particular notice." The Cromwellian period is, as has just been seen, no less a usurpation to Hallam. Hallam is, when all is said and done, a monarchist, although the merits of the monarchy are political rather than dynastic or mystical. Nor is there in England some absolute incompatibility with a republican constitution of government. After all, "the most conspicuously successful experiment of republican institutions . . . has taken place in a people of English origin."[42]

The Restoration and the Revolution of 1688

After Cromwell's death, Hallam's account becomes more detailed. At times it is a plain analytical narrative and one is in danger of losing sight of the function of the work. Charles II was restored in 1660 "to nothing but the bounded prerogatives of a King of England, bounded by every ancient and modern statute, including those of the long parliament, which had been enacted for the subjects' safety." Hallam sees the restoration not as necessarily a revival of monarchism in itself; it was rather a "restoration of ancient laws and liberties."[43] And although there were cases of misgovernment in the generation after 1660, these were not through any fault of the restorers.

The static nature of the essence of the constitution underlies one aspect of Hallam's justification of the Revolution of 1688. Charles II was guilty equally with James II of aspiring to an unfettered prerogative. "It is of importance also to observe, that James II was not so misled and betrayed by false or foolish counsellors, as some would suggest, in his endeavors to subvert the laws, but acted on a plan, long since concerted, and in which he had taken a principal share." Charles's guilt is demonstrated by his repeated duplicity. His seizure of the charters of the corporations, thereby subordinating parliamentary elections to crown influence, was "the great and leading justification of that event which drove James II from the throne."[44] The revolution cannot be treated in isolation, yet Hallam's justification of it is based on both long-term constitutional grounds and more narrowly on grounds of political expediency.[45]

The revolution was the culmination not only of struggles between the Stuarts and liberty but of five hundred years of English history. It was "the termination of that contest which the house of Stuart had obstinately maintained against the liberties, and of late, against the religion of England; or rather, of that far more ancient controversy between the crown and the people which had never been wholly at rest since the reign of John." This termination broke the course of English history. The king's title became formally dependent upon parliamentary power. There had been an incompatibility in the legal position of the king with liberty. This incompatibility was exposed by Hales's case. The judges in Hales's case were probably right in declaring for the legality of the king's dispensing power. "The course of former precedents seems rather to furnish its justification. But the less untenable such a judgment in favour of the dispensing power might appear, the more necessity would men of reflection perceive of making some great change in the relations of the people towards their sovereign." Precedent and legality are thus clearly rejected. Indeed, "it was only by recurring to a kind of paramount, and what I may call hyperconstitutional law, a mixture of force and regard to the national good, which is the best sanction of what is done in revolutions," that some decisions of the convention of 1689 could be justified. "They proceeded not by the stated rules of the English government but the general rules of mankind. They looked not so much to Magna Carta, as the original compact of society, and rejected Coke and Hale for Hooker and Grotius."[46]

What the men of 1688 effected that was of lasting value was a change of spirit. Indeed, Hallam argues that there was hardly any change in the legal standing of the monarchy. "The formal and exterior character of the monarchy remained nearly the same in so complete a regeneration of the spirit." But the spell that the monarchy had cast was broken. No longer was royal power to be defended in terms of imprescriptible hereditary right. The revolution was a victory "of those principles which, in the language of the present day, are denoted liberal or constitutional, over those of absolute monarchy, or monarchy not effectually controlled by stated boundaries." This new settlement of the monarchy received authority in the Declaration of Rights which "was indissolubly connected with the revolutionary settlement, as its motive and its condition." The Act of Settlement too ensured that after Anne's death, the title of monarchy would go to the Hanoverians. Their title thus rests exclusively on the sovereignty of the legislature. "The Act of Settlement was the seal of our constitutional laws, the complement of the revolution itself and the bill of rights."[47]

In this account of the essence of the Revolution, Hallam strikes several blows at the Tory ideas of indefeasible right. Yet although the Revolution was based on the ideology of one party, the settlement was supported by both. Any sentimental idea of monarchy or undefined royal prerogative is rejected. But if the idea of a Tory or a Whig account of the years after 1688 has any meaning, then Hallam's account is decidedly partisan. His definition of Toryism was far from impartial. "The cardinal maxim of toryism is that the king ought to exercise all his lawful prerogatives without the interference or unsolicited advice even of parliament, much less of the people." In a later passage, a greater attempt at impartiality is made. Whigs and Tories both agreed in constitutional monarchy.

A favourer of unlimited monarchy was not a tory, neither was a republican a whig. Lord Clarendon was a tory, Hobbes was not; bishop Hoadley was a whig, Milton was not. But they differed mainly in this; that to a tory the constitution, inasmuch as it was the constitution, was an ultimate point, beyond which he never looked, and from which he thought it altogether impossible to swerve; whereas a whig deemed all forms of government subordinate to the public good, and therefore liable to change, when they should cease to promote that object . . . ; the whig had a natural tendency to political improvement, the tory an aversion to it . . . [the Tory] was generally hostile to the liberty of the press, and to freedom of inquiry, especially in religion; [the Whig] their friend. The principle of the one, in short, was melioration, of the other, conservation.

And Hallam's account of the activities of men who had been conventionally called Whigs is one of mitigation. The disclosures of Dalrymple and Macpherson about the subsidies received by Russell and Sidney from Louis XIV are faced. Hallam argues that their conduct was unwise rather than reprehensible. There is, he argues speciously, "some moral distinction between the acceptance of a bribe to desert or betray our principles, and that of a trifling present for acting in conformity with them." James II and William III are portrayed in the predictable roles of villain and hero. The treatment of Jeffreys is in the tradition of Burnet and Oldmixon. The Tories of 1710–14 are censured. Queen Anne is treated with little respect. "It seems rather an humiliating proof of the sway which the feeblest prince enjoys even in a limited monarchy that the fortunes of Europe should have been changed by nothing more noble than the insolence of one waiting woman and the cunning of another."[48]

The Meaning of Whiggism

One can infer some of the aspects of the meaning of Whiggism. The term is essentially English. The nineteenth-century American use of the term is derivative. Three distinct shades can be traced—historical, philosophical, and political. The Whig tradition of history goes back to the seventeenth century and its most laconic statement is in Macaulay's address to the Edinburgh electors in 1839. In this Macaulay traced the Whig party as a coherent group back to the sixteenth century. He brought down a continuous line of Whigs: the Puritan opponents of Elizabeth; opponents of Charles I, enactors of the Habeas Corpus Act, the effectors of the Revolution, and so on down to the 1830s.[49]

Although few would have seen that an interpretation of the events of the 1640s had any bearing on policy in the eighteenth and nineteenth centuries, yet Whiggism was primarily a view of the past and a clear perception of who was right and who was wrong in English history. Philosophical Whiggism is the Whiggism of *The Whig Interpretation of History*—the ex post facto justification of events.[50] In the eighteenth and nineteenth centuries it became merged with an idea of progress and inevitability of improvement. An idea—though not necessarily a knowledge—of history was required if this aspect of Whiggism was to have any application to the present day. One had to have an idea of history in order to be on the side of history. Macaulay, in his essays on Southey and Bacon, was the most eloquent exponent of this aspect. Hallam was, as we have seen, an historical Whig, but not so much a philosophical Whig. What, however, was distinctive about Hallam's Whiggism was the political scientific aspect. It consisted of an appraisal of the realities of the structure of power. The "Whiggishness" of this empiricism consisted in its being combined with the idea of a continuous constitutional spirit that dated from the thirteenth century. The weak points of this continuous tradition are strengthened, as we have seen, by an appeal either to the realities of power—as in the discussion of Cromwell's title—or to political right—as in the justification of 1688. The empiricism might be seen as expedience. Hallam certainly laid himself open to such charges. He saw that a power if established had authority by that fact alone. "Resistance to established authority can never be warrantable until it is expedient, the proverbial saying that treason never prospers because by prospering it ceases to be treason, being founded upon very good sense."[51]

Hallam's Political Whiggism

What were the consequences of Hallam's Whiggism for his ideas on politics and the constitution of his day? Throughout all his published work Hallam was a supporter of freedom of speech and of religion. He supported Catholic emancipation in the early years of the *Edinburgh Review*. His strongest attacks in his work are against the tyrannies of statesmen and churchmen. He waxes eloquent on the rise of toleration. The ends to which Hallam's empirical expediency are directed are to the preservation of liberty. This was the higher political good for which the constitution served. In his personal life, Hallam displayed an enviable openness of mind. His style of life was conservative, yet his reading and intellectual curiosity was unlimited. In his unhappy ventures into popular education one can see his temperamental conservatism struggling with his concern for extending this liberty.

Hallam's conservatism was strengthened by an attachment to what he saw and had traced as the constitution. The change of spirit effected by the Revolution led to the actual and not just the theoretic sovereignty of Parliament. This rise of Parliament was traced as a continuous process from the reign of Charles II. Although the leaders of the Cavalier Parliament were, "in general, very corrupt men . . . they knew better than to quit the power which made them worth purchase. Thus the house of commons matured and extended those rights of inquiring into and controlling the management of public affairs, which had caused so much dispute in former times." Control and management of the executive was brought about by the principle of appropriation of supplies to limited purposes; and hence, the idea of public accountability. It was a short step from this to the doctrine of ministerial responsibility. This was effected first by impeachment. In impeaching Danby in 1679, the commons "went a great way towards establishing the principle that no minister can shelter himself behind the throne by pleading obedience to the orders of his sovereign. He is answerable for the justice, the honesty, the utility of all measures emanating from the crown, as well as for their legality." In spite of this novelty, Hallam asserts that in the reign of William III responsibility is required by "the spirit of the constitution."[52]

Hallam's Later View of the Constitution

Hallam thought that the constitution reached its zenith after 1688. This perfection was destroyed by the Reform Act of 1832, which Hallam opposed. He wrote to his young friend, Lord Mahon, in 1835, "Our practical constitution from 1688 to 1831 I hold to be among the best and happiest that has existed." The Reform Act made the constitution more democratic and other institutions were in danger of being destroyed. The following year he explained further objections to Reform to Lord Mahon. By making the constitution more popular, the balance of political power would change. "It cannot be many years before the great commercial towns will press for a larger share of the representation. . . . Adopt the numerical standard as the reform bill did & how can you stop? . . . Surely the centre of gravity must descend, and we shall have no equilibrium till the political ascendancy falls to those who possess so many of the social & physical sources of power." There were other alarming indications of the spread of the democratic spirit outside Parliament. "It is plain that the conservative party is driven to work on the passions of the people as much as their opponents." Why, in spite of all this, was the "constitution" not overturned? The answer lies in the fact that an equilibrium of the constitution was being maintained by a force countervailing that of the people.

I am more & more inclined to hope for better things than I once did in case of its overthrow . . . we may reasonably hope that, after some experience of the impossibility of governing by the whole body of their attorneys, in parliament, a stronger executive will be framed, than at present we are inclined to hear, & the want of which seems the great practical evil of the actual state of things. I admit that this will probably leave the house of peers in the lurch, . . . I do not however anticipate such a revolution in under twenty years."[53]

It would be rash to claim Hallam as a prophet of the modern omnicompetent state on the strength of this one passage. Yet the ideas implicit do provide a bridge between two apparently incompatible interpretations of the English constitution: the classical accounts of De Lolme and Blackstone and the modern interpretations where the machinery of government administration is appreciated as a power dominating the parliamentary and legal processes, interpretations that were heralded by Walter Bagehot and A. V. Dicey.

Chapter Four
Literary History

Background of *Literary History* in England

Henry Hallam's *Introduction to the Literary History of Europe in the Fifteenth, Sixteenth and Seventeenth Centuries* was published in two parts: the first volume in 1837, the last three in 1839. Hallam thought he was supremely suited to be the author of the work. "I cannot afford to doubt," he concluded the work, "that I have contributed something to the general literature of my country, something to the honourable estimation of my own name and to the inheritance of those, if it is for me still to cherish that hope, to whom I have to bequeath it."[1]

Literary history in Britain was not, in the 1830s, an established historiographical form. The form can be traced back to the Elizabethans, but, by the eighteenth century there were four different approaches to the subject. In the first place there was the biographical method with its supreme achievement, Dr. Johnson's *Lives of the Poets*. This was an advancement on an earlier method of a catalog of writers. Biographical criticism placed the work in the context of a life and was literary history inasmuch as it related to something outside the text itself. Second, there was the anthology that might also include a criticism and a discussion of the interconnection of writers and writings. An outstanding example of this was Walter Scott's *Border Minstrelsy*. Third, there was the survey of literature sometimes included in the more general histories. David Hume subordinated unimaginative biographies of writers to the end of his chapters on a particular reign. They were in a section entitled "Miscellaneous Transactions of the Reign"—a ragbag that included anything from ladies' fashions to the price of corn. Robert Henry, in his *History of Great Britain,* developed Hume's plan in his division of each reign into many subjects. Fourth, there were the historians of literature themselves. "The first historian of English literature in the full sense of the term," says René Wellek, was Thomas Warton (1728–90).[2] Warton's *History of English*

Poetry, which extended only to the end of the sixteenth century, was a work of great erudition. It was not original but it was the completion of a task that had attracted but eluded both Pope and Gray.

Hallam derived inspiration for his work, however, not so much from British predecessors as from continental and, more particularly, German scholarship. In his preface he acknowledges his debts to other scholars. A universal history of modern arts and science was projected in Germany in the 1790s. The authors of some of the volumes— Bouterwek on poetry and polite letters; Bühle on speculative philosophy; Kästner on mathematics; Heeren on classical philology—are among the most frequently cited of Hallam's authorities. A further major source was a contemporary of Hallam—the Genevan, Jean Charles Leonard Simonde de Sismondi, a friend of Madame de Staël and a brother-in-law of Sir James Mackintosh. Sismondi published his *Littérature du Midi* in 1813. None of these works was available in English before 1837. Hallam felt the need for such a work as his own in the English language. He offered his volumes to the public not "as a book of reference on particular topics . . . but . . . as an entire and synoptical work."[3]

Form of the Work

These are considerable claims, but they are justified insofar as the work is a pioneer. It was admired in its day for its astonishing erudition, and Disraeli even took the work with him on his honeymoon.[4] It seems, however, that the reasons for the work's neglect outside the ranks of literary historians[5] lie not so much in the content as in the scale and arrangement. Hallam had great difficulty in the presentation of his matter. How was he to divide the boundless amount of material? Chronologically or by nation or by subject? Any arrangement was bound to have drawbacks.[6] In December 1835 he wrote to Murray to say that he had finished the first volume. "The second is very nearly finished and some progress has been made with the third." From this, one may infer that the work was originally planned in three volumes. The delay, which he deplored, arose from the difficulties of scope and structure. "The practice of publishing volumes separately has now become very general and seems to promote their sales—in some respects, it is not what I like."[7] When the last three volumes were published in 1839, there are signs that volume 4 was hurried.

The first volume opens with a long chapter on literature in the Middle Ages. To some extent it supplements the last volume of Hallam's *Middle Ages*. However, whereas in that work Hallam was using literary sources to illustrate the state of society and the causes of the revival of learning, in this first chapter Hallam is more interested in the literature itself. He discusses the development of the vernacular languages, medieval universities, and the differing levels of education in the various nations of Europe. Three chapters follow dealing with all literature chronologically. The chapters after 1440 are subdivided, breaking the periods into decades. This is convenient though there are some curious results. In the decade 1510–1520, Hallam admits that "the laws of synchronism, which we have hitherto obeyed, brings strange partners together, and we pass at once from Luther to Ariosto."[8] But there is more rational method in dealing with the literature after 1520. Five chapters divide the literature of 1520–1550 into ancient literature, theological literature, philosophical literature, the "literature of taste"—including poetry, drama, and criticism—and finally scientific and miscellaneous literature.

The three later volumes are on a simpler plan. Each deals with a period of fifty years, and the literature of a particular field is distributed among the chapters as in the last part of the first volume. Some of the chapters are divided further under more specialized headings—such as jurisprudence or anatomical literature, or the work of one man such as Bacon or Grotius, or under national headings.

This rigid chronological system brings its own difficulties. Discussion of Shakespeare's work is in four places in two different volumes. A treatise by Galileo written in 1590 has to be deferred to the following volume because it was not *published* until 1632. Hallam appreciated these difficulties, but he wanted to avoid "any tabular arrangement of literature such as has often been attempted with no very satisfactory result which would be absolutely inappropriate to such a work as the present, . . . and would interfere too continually with that general regard to chronology, without which the name of history seems incongruous."[9]

A further difficulty is self-imposed. Hallam wished to exclude rigorously anything but literary history. "We must not tread closely on the ground of political history nor discuss too minutely any revolutions of opinion which do not distinctly manifest themselves in literature," he says as a prologue to a discussion of the Counter-Reformation. And in a reference to the Treaty of Westphalia he apologizes that "such matters of history do not belong to us, when they do not bear a close relation to the warfare of the pen." Other weaknesses of the work are, if not self-imposed, at least planned. At times there is a particularly long discussion of and paraphrase of some work. There is no clear justification for such passages. Sometimes it is because the work is inaccessible. Thus an oration by Richard Croke on classical learning in England in the early sixteenth century is given at length because of "the great scarcity of this tract." As the poetry of the seventeenth-century French Jesuit Rapin "is not in the hands of every one who has a taste for Latin poetry," Hallam gives a specimen. Several long extracts from Grotius' letters are given. Hallam apologizes for the "very long note, which may be thought a superfluous digression in a work of mere Literature" on account of the fact that the letters "are not much read; nor are they in many public libraries. The index is also very indifferent, so that without the trouble I have taken of going over the volume, it might be very difficult to find these curious passages." Decline in reputation is also a pretext for lengthy extracts or summaries. Hallam gives a long "analysis of Cumberland's *De Legibus Naturae* because it is now very little read, and yet was of great importance in the annals of ethical philosophy." Conversely "it would be an unnecessary prolixity to offer in this place an analysis of so well-known a book as Locke's Essay on the Human Understanding. Few have turned their attention to metaphysical inquiries without reading it." Grotius is analyzed at length, however, because of the unworthy criticism of Dugald Stewart.[10]

What are the other reasons for giving attention to a work? Primarily, it is necessary to select only "such as appear, by the permanence, or, at least, the immediate lustre of their reputation, to have deserved of the great republic of letters better than the rest." But an "irksome" catalog of names is given "with no other object than that none of those who by their ability and diligence carried forward the landmarks of human knowledge, should miss, in a history of literature, of their meed of remembrance." Yet historiography is strangely excluded on the grounds that "the number of books that possess some value is excessively great, and would occupy a disproportionate place" in his work. So only "where history has been written with peculiar beauty of language, or philosophical spirit"[11] is there a comment.

Hallam's ambitious scheme is restricted by the physical impossibility of one man actually reading all the literature of three centuries. "In a work like the present, it is impossible to follow up every subject; and I think that a general reference to a book of reputation and easy accessibility is better than an attempt to abridge it." As a result, in order to be comprehensive, much is derivative. Hallam is quite frank in his dependence on other authorities. Yet a wry remark elsewhere refers to the perennial "habit of the literary world . . . to speak of books by hearsay."[12]

Science and Philosophy

In the Middle Ages, progress in either "philosophy" or "science" was only to be attained once the inductive system was accepted. In the Middle Ages, science was barbaric, a confusion of superstition, and there was but occasional advancement. The work of Roger Bacon was "strangely compounded of almost prophetic gleams of the future course of science, and the best principles of the inductive philosophy, with a more than usual credulity in the superstitions of his own time." During the following centuries, there was a gradual disappearance of the superstition. Men were less disposed to accept things on authority and more inclined to investigate their environment. Hallam relished the useful researches of Vesalius who, with his fellow students, "prowled by night in charnel-houses, they dug up the dead from the grave, they climbed the gibbet, in fear and silence, to steal the mouldering carcase of the murderer; the risk of ignominious punishment and the secret stings of superstitious remorse, exalting no doubt the delight of these useful, but not very enviable pursuits."[13] For scientific pursuits, to be creditable, had to be useful.

Scholastic philosophy had much in common with the superstitions of medieval science. Progress could only be attained after the rubble was cleared away. Scholastic philosophy had consisted of "barbarous and unprofitable disputations which occupied Europe for some hundred years." The merit of some, such as Ramus, was "not so much founded on his own deserts, as on the effect he produced in loosening the fetters of inveterate prejudice, and thus preparing the way like many others of his generation for those who were to be the restorers of genuine philosophy."[14]

One of the earliest of the pioneers of the new "genuine" philosophy was Niccolò Machiavelli. Hallam's appreciation of him is eloquent. "The absence of all passion, the continual reference of every public measure to a distinct end, the disregard of vulgar associations with names of persons, render him though too cold of heart, for a generous reader, a sagacious and useful monitor for any one who can employ the necessary methods of correcting his theorems." This is, one suspects, how Hallam would have wished his own reputation to be appreciated.

Through all his published work, as we have seen, Hallam was on his guard against undue reverence for things, people, or institutions; a reverence inspired by the name or reputation, rather than by the authentic article. It is for this quality found in Machiavelli's writings, that Hallam applauds the Florentine. Machiavelli's contemporary, Leonardo da Vinci, gets only a casual mention in the *Literature of Europe*. His notebooks were not known in the 1830s and his paintings were irrelevant to Hallam's purposes. But in an age of dogmatism Leonardo "first laid down the grand principle of Bacon, that experiment and observation must be the guides to just theory in the investigation of nature." Yet views like these were far from general. At the beginning of the seventeenth century "the higher philosophy, which is concerned with general truth, and the means of knowing it, had been little benefitted by the labours of any modern inquiry."[15] In the remark, one can see both the close association and also the distinctive roles of philosophy and science. Philosophy was "the general truth" and "the means of knowing it" later became known as science.

Philosophy, like science, had to be useful, and the stages of utility could be measured by progress. Although Descartes and Hobbes are recognized as having cleared the way of scholastic rubble and having laid down the new philosophy, the greatest credit goes to their immediate predecessor, Francis Bacon. Bacon it was who expounded the inductive system and enabled men to make progress in science and philosophy. Yet even Bacon did not accept Galileo's solar theories. Hallam gives an outline of *The Advancement of Learning*. At the end of the analysis, Hallam notes the comparatively recent appreciation of Bacon's work. "Scotland has the merit of having led the way; Reid, Stewart, Robinson and Playfair turned that which had been blind veneration into a rational worship; and I should suspect that more have read Lord Bacon within these thirty years than in the two preceding centuries." In the 1830s a new edition of Bacon's works was published, edited by Basil Montagu: an edition that produced the famous essay on Bacon by Macaulay, an essay which Hallam calls "a very brilliant sketch of the Baconian philosophy." Bacon was seen by Hallam as comparable with "those liberators of nations, who have given them laws by which they might govern themselves and retained no homage but their gratitude."[16]

As the centuries unroll in Hallam's work, the sections on science tend to get shorter and shorter. This is because of Hallam's ignorance of the detail of the work. Indeed, most of the sections are little more than a catalog of names, books, and discoveries. In the last volume Hallam regrets "the slightness of my own acquaintance with subjects so momentous and difficult, . . . upon which I could not write without presumptuousness and much peril of betraying ignorance."[17] However, as both an historian and a Fellow of the Royal Society, Hallam does discuss the origins of that society and of similar associations in Europe.

Classical Standards of Criticism

Hallam's touch is surest when he is writing of the "literature of taste" of these centuries. As a would-be poet in his childhood, as the father of one poet and the friend or acquaintance of Wordsworth, Rogers, Tennyson, Tupper, and Macaulay, his critical observations of poetry had some authority. In criticism, Hallam was a firm classicist. He believed that there were standards of excellence and that a work should be measured by these standards alone. "It will not convert bad writing into good," he writes in castigating relativist critical praises of Caldéron, "to tell us, as is perpetually done, that we must place ourselves in the author's position, and make allowance for the taste of his age or the temper of his nation." Literary greatness was not dependent upon circumstances. "There is only one cause for the want of great men in any period: —nature does not yet think fit to produce them. They are no creatures of education and circumstance."[18] What were these standards of excellence in good writing? Hallam is much clearer in seeing the bad qualities of writing. However, from his comment on various works one is able to construct a system of critical values.

The models for excellence were from the ancient world: Cicero for prose and Homer for verses. In the early sixteenth century Italy "was the land of taste and sensibility." What constituted this taste and sensibility? Hallam tells us. "Nothing was so much at heart with the Italian scholars, as to write a Latin style, not only free from barbarism, but confinable to the standard of what is called the Augustan age, that is, of the period from Cicero to Augustus." One example of such a good writer was Bembo, who revived "that consummate grace and richness that enchants every successive generation in the periods of Cicero."

At this time, England's poverty in works of criticism was partly due to the fact that they had not "as yet drunk deep enough of classical learning to discriminate by any steady principle, the general beauties of composition." And in the middle of his unfavorable criticism of the English metaphysical poets, he makes a vigorous plea for the value of a classical education. "The best, and perhaps the only, secure basis for *public* taste, for an aesthetic appreciation of beauty, in a court, a college, a city, is so general a diffusion of classical knowledge, as by rendering the finest models familiar, and by giving them a sort of authority, will discountenance and check at the outset the vicious novelties which always exert some influence over uneducated minds." Yet it is possible to overdo "consummate grace and richness." Vossius, in his Latin writings, established "as much correctness of writing as is attainable in a dead language." Vossius showed how there were obvious words which did not occur in the writings of Cicero: "yet it would be mere affectation to avoid them." And affectation is to be avoided by people of taste. Affectation was the fault of much Spanish writing and of course is the chief charge against the metaphysical poets. What was to be sought in good writing was a refined moderation. Anglo-Saxon poetry is dismissed since "it is often turgid, and always rude." Much English literature of the sixteenth century is rude and "any comparison of the Elizabethan poetry, save Spenser's alone, with that of the 19th century would show an extravagant predilection for the mere name or dress of antiquity." But English prose of the early seventeenth century had lost much of its rudeness. "If we meet in Sidney, Hooker, or the prose of Spenser, with obsolete expressions or forms, we find none that are unintelligible, none that give offence." Rudeness, bad though it is, was something that could not always be helped.

There were other faults of commission that were best avoided: an affected pedantry, for example. Although Hallam, a prodigy of learning in his own time, has a sympathetic admiration for his counterparts of the early seventeenth century, an undue display of knowledge is to be deplored. Pedantry never marred the best models of Greece and Rome. "This was nevertheless the weed that overspread the face of literature in those ages when Greece and Rome were the chief objects of veneration." Classical learning, the education of gentlemen, led Hallam to look for good breeding in literature. The letters of Manutius were written in "a gentleman-like tone, without the virulence or querulousness that disgusts too often in the compositions of literary men." The man of gentle and moderate habits and of just and fine taste is likewise outraged by the revenge drama of the sixteenth century. "Scenes of agony and images of unspeakable sorrow, when idly accumulated by an inventor at his ease, as in many of our older tragedies, and in much of modern fiction, give offence to a reader of just taste, from their needlessly trampling upon his sensibility."[19]

Hallam on English Literature

How did the English poets fare with Hallam? He sees a wistful sadness in Elizabethan poetry due to the influence of Petrarchian melancholy, the serious nature of the Reformation, and the persecutions of Mary. Spenser is one of the greatest of English poets. He chose more pleasing themes than did his contemporaries. "It is on love and beauty, on holiness and virtue, that he reposes with all the sympathy of his soul." The *Epithalamion* is delightful. "I do not know any nuptial song, ancient or modern, of equal beauty. It is an intoxication of ecstasy, ardent, noble and pure." *The Faerie Queene* was popular from its publication. "No academy had been trained to carp at his genius with minute cavilling: no recent popularity, no traditional fame (for Chaucer was rather venerated than much in the hands of the reader) interfered with the immediate recognition of his supremacy." The first book of the poem is the best. In this "the reader has the gratification that good writing in works of fiction always produces, that of exercising his own ingenuity without perplexing it." Spenser is judged "the third name in the poetical literature of our country, . . . he has not been surpassed, except by Dante, in any other."[20]

The fall and rise of the reputation of the metaphysical poets is an interesting story in the history of taste.[21] Hallam follows Dr. Johnson and the Augustan critics in deploring their affectations. These conceits were derived from Lyly's *Euphues* and sprang "like the concetti of the Italians, and of their English imitators, from the same source, a dread of being overlooked if they paced on like their neighbours." Hallam is more severe than Johnson, however. He disagrees with Johnson in deriving the metaphysicians' style from the Italian poet Marini or the Spanish Gongora, "except as it bore marks of the same vice, a restless ambition to excite wonder by overstepping the boundaries of nature." Donne, moreover, was writing before Marini. This English poet was "the most inharmonious of our versifiers, if he can be said to have deserved such a name by lines too rugged to seem metre. Of his earlier poems many are very licentious; the latter are chiefly devout. Few are good for much; the conceits have not even the merit of being intelligible; it would perhaps be difficult to select three passages that we would care to read again."[22] This obtuseness compares with Hazlitt's reference to Donne's poetry as "some quaint riddles in verse, which the Sphinx could not unravel."[23] George Herbert's verse is not even mentioned by Hallam. The rise of Herbert's reputation started with some favorable remarks by Coleridge in *Biographia Literaria*.

Hallam on Shakespeare

There has been a similar though less dramatic variation in the appreciation of Shakespeare. The sonnets, which had long been neglected, became, in Hallam's view, too highly praised. Hallam suggests that they were addressed to a man and "the pleasure of their perusal is greatly diminished by these circumstances; and it is impossible not to wish that Shakspeare [*sic*] had never written them."[24] But Shakespeare is an enigmatic personality, individually no better known than Homer. Hallam traces the plays chronologically—which means that those dating from before 1600 are discussed in volume 2 and the rest in volume 3.[25]

Hallam does not deal with all the plays. Some of the great ones are not discussed at all. His comments are literal rather than imaginative. Like Johnson, he appreciates Shakespeare's fidelity to nature. *Two Gentlemen of Verona* has no "transgression of the probabilities of nature." *A Midsummer Night's Dream* receives high praise for its sportive fancies. "There is nothing overcharged or affectedly ornamental. Perhaps no play of Shakspeare has fewer blemishes, or is from beginning to end in so perfect keeping; none in which so few lines could be erased, or so few expressions blamed." With *The Merchant of Venice* and *As You Like It* there is a more serious note. "The philosophic eye, turned inward on the mysteries of human nature, is more and more characteristic." In *Measure for Measure* this trait is developed further. It is a play, like *Hamlet, King Lear,* and *Macbeth,* "in which Shakspeare struggles, as it were, most with the over-mastering power of his own mind; the depths and intricacies of being which he has searched and sounded with intense reflection, perplex and harass him; his personages arrest their course of action to pour forth, in language the most remote from common use, thoughts that few could grasp in the clearest expression; and thus he loses something of dramatic excellence in that of his contemplative philosophy." Hallam considers *Macbeth* to be Shakespeare's greatest play, followed by *Othello* and *King Lear.* Of these *King Lear* is analyzed. "Lear himself is perhaps the most wonderful of dramatic conceptions: ideal to satisfy the most romantic imaginations, yet idealised from the reality of nature." Hallam sees the abasement of Lear in the first act as a preparation for the intense sympathy one feels for him later on. It is in the frenzy of his grief and rage "that we find what in life may sometimes be seen, the intellectual energies grow stronger in calamity, and especially under wrong. An awful eloquence belongs to unmerited suffering." Hallam discusses none of the histories except to observe that Shakespeare "followed historical truth with considerable exactness" and that they "have identified him with English feelings in English hearts, and are very frequently read more in childhood, and better remembered than some of his superior dramas."[26]

Hallam sees Shakespeare not only as a great and imaginative poet, but as something of a censurer of mankind. This quality appears in plays like *King Lear* and *Timon of Athens* but it is seen also in the philosophic melancholy of Jaques in *As You Like It* and of the duke in *Measure for Measure.* But his greatest achievement was the variety of his creation. "The name of Shakspeare is the greatest in our literature—it is the greatest in all literature. No man ever came near to him in the creative powers of his mind; no man had ever such strength at once and such variety of imagination." He surpasses all writers of fiction— "Plautus, Cervantes, Molière, Addison, Le Sage, Fielding,

Richardson, Scott." In a review of Shakespearian criticism, Hallam observes that the current idolatry of Shakespeare has gone too far—"an extravagance rather derogatory to the critic than honourable to the poet." Hallam notes blemishes "both atrocious and contemptible" and obscurities and novelties. Addison and his contemporaries had failed to recognize his supremacy, "that unhesitating preference of him to all the world, which has become the faith of the last and the present century." It was in the frigid generation of the age of George II that Shakespeare reached his apotheosis. Garrick and the Kembles maintained the enthusiasm. Dr. Johnson's criticism "is frequently judicious but betrays no ardent admiration from Shakspeare . . . there is something magisterial in the manner wherein he dismisses each play like a boy's exercise, that irritates the reader." The multitude of second-rate critics of the previous generation was a measure of esteem for Shakespeare. "In the present century, Coleridge and Schlegel . . . gave a more philosophical and at the same time a more intrinsically exact view of Shakspeare than their predecessors."[27]

Hallam on Milton

Discussion of Milton's poetry is also fragmented because his productivity preceded and followed 1650. *Lycidas* is seen as "a test of a real feeling for what is peculiarly called poetry." Johnson's contemptuous denunciation of the poem is refuted. Johnson had thought the poem unnatural, disgusting, improbable, irreverent.[28] But such poems for Hallam "pretend to no credulity, they aim at no illusion; they are read with a willing abandonment of the imagination to a waking dream, and require only that general possibility, that combination of images which common experience does not reject as incompatible, without which the fancy of the poet would be only like that of the lunatic."[29] This defence is almost a paraphrase of Coleridge's definition of a poem in *Biographia Literaria*. In this book Coleridge explained that in the *Lyrical Ballads* he and Wordsworth had transferred "from our inward nature a human interest and a semblance of truth sufficient to procure for these shadows of imagination that willing suspension of disbelief for the moment, which constitutes poetic faith."[30]

The Concept of the Renaissance

The term "renaissance" as a periodic concept has been traced back to 1829 when a character in a short Balzac novel is said to be able to "argue fluently on Italian or Flemish painting, on the Middle Ages or on the Renaissance."[31] But this, and other examples of the use of the term, were not as significant or influential as Jules Michelet's volume in his *History of France* which he called *La Renaissance* and published in 1855. The term achieved a clarity and an autonomy as a concept in the 1860s with the publication of Burckhardt's *Civilization of the Renaissance in Italy*. Even this work took a generation to "become fully ripe for what Burckhardt had to offer" as is demonstrated by the dates of editions. The concept that emerged with the term, however, drew on many ideas, including the work of Hallam.

Hallam has no clear periodic idea of the Renaissance. However, he has many suggestions about the literature and learning of Italy in the fifteenth and sixteenth centuries being related to broader social causes. This social interpretation is first stated in the last chapter of the *Middle Ages*. In this chapter, which is partly derived from William Robertson's introduction to his *Charles the Fifth,* Hallam traces the spread of commerce in north Italy, the rise of bankers and merchants to an established social position. They were thus able to afford a patronage of the arts. This background to what Hallam, following an old tradition, calls the revival of learning is discussed further in the first chapters in *The Literature of Europe*. Among the other general causes he includes the invention of paper, "without which both the art of writing would have been much less practised, and the invention of printing serviceable to mankind."

There is a danger, Hallam argues, in seeing a gradual European ending of the Middle Ages, a danger against which he also guards in his earlier work. In the work under review Hallam thought that this "shifting of intellectual exertion from one country to another is not peculiar to the middle ages; but, in regard to them, it has not always been heeded by those who, using the trivial metaphor of light and darkness, which it is not easy to avoid, have too much considered Europe as a single point under a receding or advancing illumination." But it was Italy that was the source for the revival of classical learning.

"We have the greatest reason to doubt whether without the Italians of these ages [early fifteenth century] it would ever have occurred." By concentrating on a revival of learning, by his reluctance to see a gradual and irrevocable process, Hallam sees the fifteenth-century revival as nothing new. "Taking Europe generally, far from being in a more advanced stage of learning at the beginning of the 15th century, than two hundred years before, she had, in many respects, gone backwards."[32]

What caused the revival of ancient learning in Italy? The Italians had for generations identified themselves with the Romans, and there were various traditions that kept this identification alive such as the study of the civil law. "The monuments of ancient Italy were perpetual witnesses; their inscriptions were read; it was enough that a few men like Petrarch should animate the rest; it was enough that learning should become honourable, and that there should be the means of acquiring it. The story of Rienzi, familiar to everyone, is a proof that enthusiasm could be kindled by ancient recollections." Cities became wealthier and the people better educated. "A style of painting appeared in the works of Giotto and his followers, rude and imperfect according to the skilfulness of later times, but in itself pure, noble and expressive and well adapted to reclaim the taste from extravagance of romance to classic simplicity."[33] Furthermore, the habit of writing Latin was maintained by the learned who rarely resorted to the vernacular.

Thus Hallam's definition of the revival of letters was restricted to a discovery of taste and of that excellence which is found only in classical models. The revival of learning was due to social causes as well as to the incidental existence of great men. In spite of Hallam regarding the image of "light and darkness" as trivial and trite, yet he uses an analogous simile in writing of the work of Pope Nicholas V and in comparing him with Gregory I. "These eminent men, like Michael Angelo's figures of Night and Morning seem to stand at the two gates of the middle ages, emblems and heralds of the mind's long sleep, and of its awakening."[34] There was something new and luminous about the fifteenth century. It was like the dawn of a day that would continue into his own times. The era of the revival of letters was contemporary with the world of modern Europe.

Hallam and the Reformation

The other concept of the period between 1400 and 1700 that became part of the historiography of modern Europe was the Reformation. Hallam approached "this subject with some hesitation, well aware that impartiality is no protection against unreasonable cavilling: ". . . it is not required, however, in a work of this nature, to do much more than state shortly the grounds of dispute and the changes wrought in the public mind." Hallam succeeds pretty well in his aim. He apportions praise and blame, without regard to theological party, and his general interpretation is favorable to neither Catholics, Lutherans, nor Calvinists. He sees antecedents to the Reformation in the fifteenth century. The monks had long been disliked, popular preaching had grown up in Germany, and theological tracts had issued forth in a great stream from the presses in the Rhine and Neckar valleys. Erasmus in particular castigated many of the abuses of the church. "Thus every thing was prepared for the blow to be struck by Luther." Indeed, the German nation was so aware of the abuses of the church that "if neither Luther nor Zwingle [*sic*] had ever been born, there can be little question that a great religious schism was near at hand." Luther, however, was the instrument of the Reformation. Hallam does not like Luther and indeed his picture of the man aroused some criticism. Hallam goes so far as to quote Bossuet with approval on Martin Luther. Luther, by his emphasis on justification by faith alone, implied the irrelevance of a good life. It should be seen, furthermore, that "the doctrines of Luther, taken altogether, are not more rational, that is, conformable to what man, a priori, would expect to find in religion, than those of the church of Rome." While recognizing the greatness of his translation of the Bible, Hallam is severe on Luther's Latin work. "Their intemperance, their coarseness, their inelegance, their scurrility, their wild paradoxes that menace the foundations of religious morality" mar them, and his reply to Henry VIII "can be described as little else than bellowing in bad Latin."[35]

The Reformer who does appeal to Hallam, however, is Melanchthon. Whenever he appears in Hallam's pages there is a warm glow of approval. Melanchthon became "not only one of the great lights of the

Reformation, but, far above all others, the founder of general learning"
in Germany. And when Melanchthon died, "a literary decline com-
menced, slow but uniform and permanent."[36]

Hallam is very careful to point out that the Reformation in itself had
nothing to do with liberty.[37] The argument that the Reformation was a
stage in the rise of liberty was an old one, and reached its most eloquent
expression in 1865 with the *History of Rationalism* by the youthful W. E.
H. Lecky. "It is one of the fallacious views of the Reformation to fancy
that it sprang from any notion of political liberty, in such a sense as we
attach to the word." There was no religious freedom, no right of private
judgment. "The Reformation was a change of masters; a voluntary one,
no doubt, in those who had any choice; and in this sense, an exercise, for
the first time, of their personal judgment. But no-one having gone over
to the confession of Augsburg, or that of Zurich was deemed at liberty
to modify those creeds at his pleasure." And as for the second period of
the Reformation, "those ominous symptoms which had appeared in its
earlier stage, disunion, virulence, bigotry, intolerance, far from yield-
ing to any benignant influence, grew more inveterate and incurable."
Even Melanchthon, "tolerant by nature, and knowing enough of the
spirit of persecution which disturbed his peace, was yet unfortunately
led by timidity to express, in a letter to Beza, his approbation of the
death of Servetus."[38]

Yet there is also a view Hallam had of the Reformation that seems to
be inconsistent with the idea that the Reformation had nothing to do
with liberty; inconsistent, that is, unless one realizes that Hallam saw
democracy and liberty as incompatible. This view occurs several times
in Hallam's chapters on the religious crisis of the sixteenth century. It is
that there is a close analogy between those times and his own. The
fifteenth-century councils, in which in the *Middle Ages* he had seen "the
whig principles of the church," "were to the Reformation what the
parliament of Paris was to the French Revolution." And in his general
comments on the Reformation he observes:

We cannot give any attention to the story of the Reformation, without being
struck by the extraordinary analogy it bears to that of the last fifty years. He
who would study the spirit of this mighty age may see it reflected as in a
mirror from the days of Luther and Erasmus. In each, the characteristic
features are a contempt for antiquity, a shifting of private judgment in the

most uninformed, a sanguine confidence in the amelioration of human affairs, a fixing of the heart on great ends, with a comparative disregard of all things intermediate. In each there has been so much of alloy in the motives, and, still more, so much of danger and suffering in the means, that the cautious and moderate have shrunk back, and sometimes retraced their own steps, rather than encounter evils which at a distance they had not seen in their full magnitude. Hence we may pronounce with certainty what Luther, Hutton, Carlstadt, what again More, Erasmus, Melanchthon, Cassander would have been in the 19th century, and what our own contemporaries would have been in their times.

And optimism as to the inevitability of democracy in the nineteenth century was to be checked by the memory of the Counter-Reformation and the dashing of hopes of the Protestants of 1560. "The late rush of many nations towards democratical opinions has not been so rapid and so general as the change of religion about that period."[39]

The Counter-Reformation and the Rise of Freedom

The Counter-Reformation is described at some length. Like the eighteenth-century Scottish historian Robertson, Hallam was fascinated by the Jesuits. While there could be no suspicion of an ideological sympathy, yet there was a sneaking admiration for them. "Men saw in the Jesuits courage and self-devotion, learning and politeness; qualities the want of which had been the disgrace of monastic fraternities." "Whatever might be objected . . . to their system of casuistry, whatever want of scrupulousness they may have shown in their conduct, they were men who never swerved from the path of labour, and, it might be, suffering in the cause which they deemed that of God." Yet this single-minded devotion to the papacy cannot appeal to those that are troubled by the conflict of particular duties in promoting the public good; "hence the little confidence we repose in enthusiasts, even when, in a popular mode of speaking, they are most sincere." The Jesuits revived a Scholastic way of arguing and took great pains in education. Their extension of auricular confession led to casuistry and the formulation of rules for extenuating circumstances in absolving those who confess. Bossuet's *Variations of Protestant Churches* also strikes a sympathetic chord in Hallam's heart. "Never did his genius find a subject more fit to display its characteristic impetuosity, its arrogance, or its cutting and merciless spirit of sarcasm." But the fallacy of his case is brought forward. "The essential fallacy of Romanism, that truth must ever exist visibly on earth, is implied in the whole strain of Bossuet's attack on the variances of protestantism: it is evident that variance of opinion proves error somewhere; but unless it can be shown that we have any certain method of excluding it, this should only lead us to be more indulgent towards the judgment of others, and less confident of our own."[40]

Slowly the idea of toleration emerged—but only incidentally and as a consequence of bargain and compromise. Some events are wrongly seen as landmarks in toleration. "The edict of Nantes was a compromise between belligerent parties; the toleration of the dissidents in Poland was nearly of the same kind; but no state powerful enough to restrain its sectaries from the exercise of their separate worship had any scruples about the right and obligation to do so." Some English writers suggested toleration, such as Hales and the "immortal" Chillingworth. But Jeremy Taylor in his *Liberty of Prophesying* is the first "who sapped and shook the foundations of dogmatism and pretended orthodoxy; the first who taught men to seek peace in unity of spirit rather than of belief; and, instead of extinguishing dissent, to take away its sting by charity, and by a sense of human fallibility."[41] Taylor's work was full of great learning, repetitive and luxuriant erudition. But it was not until the expulsion of Protestants from France in 1685 that the question of liberty of conscience was brought home to many and men like Bayle and Locke laid a broader foundation for religious toleration.

The Strengths and Weakness of the Work

Hallam's last great work has many of his characteristic qualities. In writing of George Saintsbury's apparently limitless knowledge of books Oliver Elton wrote of that man's "omnilegence."[42] This quality was shared by Henry Hallam. Hallam's omnilegence makes him a cosmopolitan guide through three centuries of European literature of the most varied kind. He is free of any nationalistic partisanships. The work differs from his two earlier works in being more detailed, "antiquarian" rather than "philosophical." He has read some of the erudite modern Germans and, in writing his book, is showing some of their influence both in method and in spirit. He shows a qualified admiration for the new criticism of Herder and Schlegel.[43]

His style, frequently circuitous with qualifications and enigmatic begging of questions, reveals a wry humor that is less obvious in his earlier works. Pope Julian, for example, devised a new calendar which was adopted at once by all Catholic countries. "The protestant countries came much more slowly into the alteration; truth being no longer truth, when promulgated by the Pope." In discussing Sir Philip Sidney's *Arcadia,* Hallam quotes from Horace Walpole's remark that it is a "tedious lamentable pedantic pastoral romance which the patience of a young virgin in love cannot now wade through." Hallam doubts "whether Walpole could altogether estimate the patience of a reader so extremely unlike himself."[44]

The work, however, has faults. One feels that an opportunity has been missed. One goes through a great catalog of writers, neatly and sensibly arranged. But one cannot see the wood for the trees, or the literature for the books. Occasionally Hallam pauses to discuss "the general state of literature," but this is a list of learned societies, of libraries or the number of printing presses in operation. Only with the theological literature is there any relation between literature and society—although one may also except a few pages on the English stage and its relation to English society.

Altogether Hallam's *Introduction to the Literature of Europe in the Fifteenth, Sixteenth and Seventeenth Centuries* was a pioneering work in Britain. It has been praised by discriminating critics for over a century. And, to a large extent, unlike his other works, it has not been superseded by any other single work.

Chapter Five

Hallam's Place in Historical Literature

Hallam's Undergraduate Reading

Hallam's literary influences were largely the British historians of the previous two centuries. He fits easily into a tradition, and the decline in his posthumous reputation can be explained by the decline in "philosophical history." Before we consider the decline and fall of this mode of history, we can consider, from the evidence of some of Hallam's notebooks, the historian's early reading.

In the summer of 1797 he embarked on Gibbon's works starting with the autobiography, and read Adam Smith's *Wealth of Nations*. He began this last work by reading the first seventy pages; the following day he reread the first seventy and then read the next thirty; the next day he reread those thirty and on to another fifty—and so on through the whole book. Then, having read it, he spent four more days looking over parts of the work. This careful examination of Smith's work gave Hallam "some notion of Political Economy; a vast & important study, in which I hope one day to make further advances." Smith's book, at this time twenty-one years old, was an unlikely work for an undergraduate to read so meticulously.[2]

During the following winter he started to read Blackstone in the same systematic manner as he had read Adam Smith. And in the summer of 1798 he was reading English history.

On the 2d, 3d and 4d of July I read Henry, Hume and Rapin to the year 1527. From this to the 9th of August inclusive I read Burnet's History of the reformation, omitting the collection of records; with Henry and Andrews' continuation, Hume and Rapin to the death of Mary in 1558. From this to the 25th of August inclusive I read the remainder of Burnet, Camden's

Annals of Elizabeth with Andrews' continuation, Hume and Rapin to 1603. From this time I take it up in a larger scale, the reigns of the Stuarts are highly important both in a legal and political view & from the Revolution I mean to omit no opportunity of increasing my knowledge upon this spiritual study.

Thus it can be seen that Hallam's private studies as an undergraduate included the standard historical and political classics of the late seventeenth and eighteenth centuries—Gibbon, Adam Smith, Blackstone, Hume, Rapin, and Burnet. But during his maturity Hallam read intensively—as can be seen from the references in his works.

Philosophical History

The inspiration for philosophical history was due partly to European works such as those of Montesquieu, Voltaire, and Giannone. The method was also partly due to a development in the style of writing history. In the seventeenth century, history usually consisted of a paraphrase of old chronicles. If the chronicles were to be accepted or challenged in the light of any archival discoveries, then the challenge was subordinated—as, for example, in the work of Brady—to the preface. In the period from 1660 to 1730, there were published many public records of the Middle Ages, and the commentaries that improved historical interpretation were in the notes or prefaces.[3] These publications of records were often promoted and read for the sake of partisan zeal. After 1730, however, partisan issues died down but the contrast between the published documents and the prefaces remained. The successor of the preface was the philosophical history. The major historians of the eighteenth century disdained the antiquarian piling of detail upon detail. Richard Gough suggested a definition of "history" in 1770 in the first number of *Archaeologia,* the journal of the Society of Antiquaries: "The arrangement and proper use of facts is HISTORY; —not a mere narrative taken up at random and embellished with poetic diction, but a regular and elaborate inquiry into every ancient record and proof, that can elucidate or establish them." It was, on the other hand, the task of the antiquary to supply "materials to those who have sagacity or leisure to extract from the common mass whatever may answer useful purposes."[4] Or, as Edward Gibbon more bluntly put it,

"The part of an historian is as honourable as that of a mere chronicler or compiler of gazettes is contemptible."[5]

These were the attitudes of mind that characterized the philosophical historians. The wish to separate the truth from the facts, the aim, as one historian put it, "not so much as to load [the reader's] memory as to enrich his understanding, to elevate his thoughts, and even to captivate his affection,"[6] led to some distinctive features. There was a precious intellectualism in the writing of history. Evidence was used to argue a point. There was a love of paradox, of irony, and of skepticism about religious enthusiasm. The writing of history was a didactic exercise, a moral fable based on the evidence of the past.[7] The historian had to point out that things were not always as they seemed. He had to distill the essence from the form. It has been shown how Hume derived England's freedom from the Puritans whose principles appeared so frivolous and habits so ridiculous. Hallam himself sees Charles II's mistresses as important agents in the story of the progressive improvement of the constitution. The past was subordinated to the historian's intelligence or to his function as an educator. This meant that some aspects of the past were more important than others. Hallam shared the philosophical patronizing disdain for the period of European history before the sixteenth century.

The Eighteenth Century and the Middle Ages

The eighteenth century was not such an undistinguished century for medieval studies as is sometimes believed, although medieval scholarship after 1730 did tend to go against the grain of conventional taste. In the early years of the century, there was still a feverish activity among antiquarians in publishing documents of medieval transactions. A legal concern for precedent led men to go to the past in order to find the answers to contemporary problems. Charles II's struggle with his last parliaments, the Revolution of 1688 and the *raison d'être* of the non-Jurors all stimulated medieval studies. But after 1730 there was a change. The Lockeian idea of social contract rendered irrelevant the search for contemporary rights in the past. After 1714 the relation between patronage and scholarship changed. There was little point and less attraction in glorifying a German dynasty. Those who found a Tory view of monarchy in medieval precedent were not inclined to apply their conclusions to the dull "usurping" Hanoverian regime. The smoother relations between church and state no longer provoked arguments which—like those of Collier and Burnet—incidentally had added enormously to people's knowledge of the medieval past. Thus the study of the Middle Ages lacked any compelling urgency.

What became most esteemed in taste was derived from the ancient world or from modern interpretations of ancient culture. The intervening period was an unfortunate "middle age." It was the "Goths" who helped to destroy Rome. So "Gothic" became synonymous with barbarous. These "Middle Ages" were of no relevance to didactic historians. History was a tool of education. To Bolingbroke it was a preparation for statesmanship, for Chesterfield a preparation for diplomacy. It was Bolingbroke who wrote: "To be ignorant about these ages which precede this era [1500] would be shameful. Nay, some indulgence may be had to a temperate curiosity in the review of them. But to be learned about them is a ridiculous affectation in any man, who means to be useful to the present age."[8] Even the Society of Antiquaries was censured by a Fellow for its interest in medieval antiquities. "I myself had admired [i.e., marveled at]," he complained, "the barbarous Dullness and Stupidity in all the Gothick contrivances of any kind. These barbarians had the originals in full perfection and yet could discover no beauties for their imitation: but Goths will always have a Gothick taste."[9] The eighteenth-century historians with widest appeal all scorned the Middle Ages. Modern Europe, which saw the emergence of a balance of power and an interdependence of European nations, was the field of study fit for the potential man of affairs. Greece and Rome, too, provided plenty of materials for instruction.

Decline of Philosophical History

Philosophical history was not without its critics in the eighteenth century. A tradition of antiquarian scholarship persisted. Dr. Johnson was suspicious of the philosophers, perhaps because most of them were Scottish. "We must consider how very little history there really is," Boswell records him as saying in 1775, "I mean real authentick history. That certain kings reigned and certain battles were fought, we can depend on as true; but all the colouring, all the philosophy of history is conjecture." On another occasion, Johnson was drawn to comment on

the work of Robertson: "He who describes what he never saw, draws
from fancy. . . . You must look upon Robertson's work as romance and
try it by that standard. History it is not."[10]

Similarly, at the end of the century there were instances of the
dominant disdain for the Middle Ages being rejected. A large Anglo-
Saxon dictionary was published in 1772. In 1778 Gilbert Stuart, a great
critic of William Robertson, argued, in *View of Society in Europe,* that
"the spirit of English history was the survival of the spirit of primitive
times." The implication of this is clear. The Middle Ages was a fit field
for enquiry. Stuart asked "Are we never to dig up the riches of the
middle times?" And, around the turn of the century, other writers,
whose works were "philosophical," were looking at Anglo-Saxon times
with sympathy. Sharon Turner wrote at length on the Anglo-Saxons,
stressing the importance of *Beowulf*, and in 1803 William Godwin, in
his *Life of Chaucer,* urged the study of the "language of our ancestors. . . . A study at least as improving as that of the language of
Greece and Rome." Whitaker, in his *Principal Corrections* [to his *History
of Manchester*] had called the pre-Conquest period "the great seed plot of
our national history."[11] John Lingard, a Roman Catholic, took up the
hint and published the *Antiquities of the Anglo Saxon Church* in 1806, a
work highly critical of the attitudes of the eighteenth century. "To have
been praised by monastic historians," he suggested ironically, "is, in
the estimation of modern writers, the infallible criterion of demerit."[12]

Lingard's defense of monastic historians and implicitly of the
"Catholic" Middle Ages illustrated one of the dangers inherent in
medieval antiquity. The Middle Ages were a battleground. Centuries of
Protestant propaganda had cast suspicion on any sympathy with the
medieval church and its culture. From the sixteenth century, antiquarians were suspected—and sometimes rightly so—of a nostalgia for the
old faith. These suspicions lasted into the nineteenth century. Indeed,
in the early nineteenth century, Joseph Milner, historian of Winchester
and one of the earliest self-conscious Gothic revivalist architects; Joseph
Berington, historian of medieval literature; Sir Henry Englefield, an
amateur medievalist and president of the Society of Antiquaries were all
Roman Catholics, as well as John Lingard. This approach reached its
peak in the work of the younger Pugin and, in particular, in his
Contrasts, published in 1836.

The outbreak of the French Revolution and the subsequent generation of war with France affected both the prevailing view of the Middle Ages and suspicion of Roman Catholics. The Revolution was undeniably "modern." To men such as Burke it seemed to be the consequence of modern ideologies—the rationalism of the eighteenth century. Sympathy with the French upper classes led to a less hostile attitude to the French church, for priests as well as aristocrats were among the émigrés. The conversion of cathedrals into Temples of Reason made Englishmen more sympathetic to French Catholicism. Sympathy passed by association to priests and monks, and by no great leap to the Middle Ages. As Hallam himself expressed it in 1827: "in some, the love of antiquity produces a sort of fanciful illusion, and the very sight of those buildings so magnificent in their prosperous hour, so beautiful even in their present ruin, begets a sympathy for those who founded and inhabited them."[13] Moreover the restriction on continental travel turned men with wanderlust to England. People discovered that England, too, had marvellous monasteries and medieval churches. In the years after 1789 there can be perceived a quickening interest in Gothic architecture. Concern for the Gothic led to a violent controversy in the 1790s when Wyatt restored Salisbury Cathedral—a controversy unimaginable half a century earlier. Many numbers of the *Gentlemen's Magazine* had a paper on Gothic architecture. Richard Gough published his great *Sepulchral Monuments of Great Britain* between 1780 and 1796. John Carter published over a period of thirty years many informed books of views of buildings. John Pinkerton was such an uncritical spokesman for the Gothic that he attributed even Stonehenge to the "Goths." In 1798 the first *History of Gothic Architecture in England* was published by Bentham and Wills. In the early years of the new century the journalist, John Britton, met a demand of the travelers in search of Gothic and produced periodically his *Beauties of England* county by county.

This was the background to the cult of the Gothic novels which, like Britton's *Beauties,* met a hungry market. Horace Walpole, no mean antiquarian himself,[14] wrote *The Castle of Otranto* in 1764. Gothic novels with their improbabilities and their anachronisms have been derided. The more conscientious and better informed historical realism practiced by Scott and his successors and the rise of the historical novel in the nineteenth century have made the Gothic tales seem quaint and picturesque horror stories. But the magic and the bizarre in the works of Horace Walpole, Clara Reeve, Mrs. Radcliffe, and M. G. Lewis can be defended. As Scott observed, Horace Walpole detailed "supernatural incidents as they would have been readily believed and received in the eleventh and twelfth centuries."[15] The novelist writing about the remote past had a general problem of how to combine authenticity with communicability. Why should the writer point out that he does not believe in the superstitions maintained by his fictional characters? "Ghosts and witches," Scott wrote in his essay on Mrs. Radcliffe, "and the whole tenets of superstition having once, and at no late period, been matter of universal belief, warranted by legal authority, it would seem no great stretch on the reader's credulity to require him, while reading of what his ancestors did, to credit for the time what those ancestors devoutly believed."[16] Scott faced these problems in his own writings, both in those dealing with the Middle Ages and in his great novels on seventeenth-and eighteenth-century Scotland. His imaginative sympathy was itself irrelevant to a didactic rejection of the remoter past. It became possible to consider the Middle Ages on their own terms and not through the distorting glasses of philosophical history. Scott's description of *things*—armor, the dress of peasants of long ago, the geological and antiquarian descriptions brought home to readers an immediacy, a sense of involvement with the remoter past. They were the literary counterpart to the pilgrimages to Fountains Abbey and to the collections of armor and of medieval things of Sir John Soane and of Jonathan Oldbuck.

These new interests all had one thing in common. It brought people into a more intimate relationship with the evidence—physical and imaginative—of the past. No longer was it necessary to treat history as an intellectual problem. The skepticism of David Hume was merrily satirized by Richard Whately in his pamphlet of 1819, *Historic Doubts Relative to Napoleon Buonaparte.*

The Opening-up of the Archives

The evidence of the past was mostly preserved among the public records which were, in the early nineteenth century, in a scandalously neglected condition in England.[17] In the eighteenth century,

Robertson, Dalrymple, Mrs. Macaulay, and Carte all looked at unpublished materials, either of government archives abroad or among private collections at home. It was not until the early nineteenth century, however, that it was generally felt that historical observations ought to be much more firmly and immediately based on unpublished and often largely unexplored authorities. One of the first major fruits of this renewed archive work was the *History of England* by John Lingard, published in eight volumes between 1819 and 1830. Lingard was scornful of what "has been called the philosophy of history, but might with more propriety be called the philosophy of romance."[18] Lingard resolved "to take nothing on trust; to confine my researches, in the first instance, to original documents and the more ancient writers; and only to consult the modern historians when I had satisfied my own judgment and composed my own narrative."[19] Accordingly he searched the State Paper Office for his sources and on a European visit in 1817 went through archives in Paris, Milan, and Rome. He even sent a friend to Simancas in Spain.

Lingard's work was bound to be inadequate. An enormous miscellany of legal, ecclesiastical, and juridical documents were housed in the Tower of London, at the Rolls Chapel, and at about sixty other offices in London. But they were in an unindexed, uncataloged state: some papers were being eaten by rats and mice, others were bound together in sacks and were rotting with damp. In 1800 a Records Commission had been set up to organize the wealth of material and to publish important parts. The Commission was renewed in 1806, 1817, 1821, 1825, and 1831. Some valuable work was done, such as the publication of the calendars of the Cottonian Library (1802), the Harleian manuscripts (1808–12), and the Lansdowne manuscripts (1819). But access to the manuscripts was obstructed by exorbitant fees and uncooperative officials. Nicholas Harris Nicolas, lawyer and historian, wrote articles in the *Westminster Review* and in his own *Retrospective Review* and also a series of pamphlets exposing the state of the public records. In one office the records were alleged to be "in a state of inseparable adhesion to the stone walls; there were numerous fragments which had only just escaped entire consumption by vermin; and were in the last stages of putrefaction."[20]

Hallam was a member of the last commission and, indeed, acted as an auditor on three occasions. In 1836 he gave evidence to a Select

Committee of the House of Commons inquiring into the work of the
Royal Commissions on Public Records. Hallam was complacent about
the state of the records, as indeed he had been in a published letter of
1833.[21] He considered the publications of the Commission valuable,
but when asked about the state of the apartments housing the records,
he told the chairman, Charles Buller, "From what I have seen, they are
in some offices very good, and in others but indifferent."[22] In his own
works, Hallam had for the most part used only published sources. The
unpublished authorities used were generally papers to which he had
easy access in the British Museum. He had no sense of the urgency or
importance of a thorough reform of the system. The Select Committee
reported to the House of Commons in 1836 and legislation followed in
1838—the Public Records Act, which completely rationalized and
improved the access to and arrangement of documents. The publication
of documents was discontinued. Yet the demand for published documents persisted and found expression in a number of small societies. In
1838 three young Cambridge men started the Camden Society with the
intention of publishing collections of records and historical documents
by subscription. The aim of one hundred subscribers was exceeded
within a few months and by 1840 the Society had over 1,200 members.[23] The scope of the Camden Society publications was general and
other smaller societies were founded with similar though with more
limited aims. These societies prospered during the 1840s and 1950s
until the government reentered the field in 1858 with the first publication of the Rolls Series.[24]

By the middle of the century a new apparatus of scholarship was
established: access to the records was easier, the care of documents
improved, and the editions of published documents were generally in
accordance with the new canons of scholarship. The climate of historical
work was transformed. The industrious though unsystematic approach
of a man like Hallam gave way to the rigorous methods of a man like
Stubbs. In the 1850s Oxford and Cambridge set up history schools,[25]
and it became as essential for an historian to have an appropriate
training before he practiced as it was for an architect.[26]

Conclusion

Thus it can be seen that while Hallam was writing, developments in
range and perspective were taking place that were to overtake his work.

Hallam's methods, as have been demonstrated, were akin to the eighteenth century. He sought to be detached, above the scene, to be—like his own hero, Hooker—judicious. Three facets of his life and work illustrate this attitude. Hallam was not an aristocrat but he lived among aristocrats and had, in some ways, an ideally aristocratic view of the world. He looked *de haut* on the conflicts and controversies of mankind. He took a similar attitude to the business of grubbing around among public records. His remarks about antiquarians suggest a social disdain. This disdain became apparent also when Hallam became briefly involved in the rough-and-tumble of educational politics around 1830. The gathering of evidence was the task of others. His was the nobler task of exercising judgment on the assembled evidence. Another facet that encouraged this tendency was his personality. Hallam was shy, unwilling to expose his feelings and anxious to appear detached, calm and aloof. There was a struggle in this, for in his early manhood his great learning led him to be somewhat impetuous and wordy in argument—the "Bore Contradictor." Yet this was placed in check and as he grew older he grew into the persona of ideal "philosopher"— learned, wise, with high ideals, sympathetic, encouraging—the Hallam as seen by Henry Holland, George Ticknor, J. L. Motley, Lord Mahon, and W. E. Gladstone, the "Patriarch of Whig history."[27] In his immediate family circle, however, Hallam was something of a martinet. There seems to have been an attempt to extend the dignity and discipline he imposed on himself to his family.

The third facet of his work was his style. The style is very consciously classical and reads—at times—like a translation of Cicero. There is a detachment in this, a rhetorical weighing of words. Hallam's attitude to history and his style are suitably matched. In his *Literature of Europe,* it has been seen that he had severe classical standards and that a writer's work was to be measured by these. Judging Hallam by his own measure, it can be seen that he aspired to an ideal style. There is a classical eloquence that seems remote from other English—the English of everyday life, of novels, of newspapers. Thus Hallam's writing is somewhat stilted. It lacks furthermore the warmth and fire of Macaulay and Carlyle, both of whom used the stylistic techniques of the novel. Hallam's style may thus deter the reader. But it has advantages of precision. The reader only gets to the core of Hallam with patience and time, but the effort is worth while, and he will see the thinking of a careful, accurate, and painstaking man looking at history from the point of view of the early nineteenth century, assailed by the impact of the French Revolution, of romanticism, and of changing intellectual horizons.

Notes and References

Preface

1. See John Vincent *The Foundation of the Liberal Party 1857–1868* (London: Constable, 1966), p. xxix.

2. See Maurice's address, "English History [to the Working Men's College]," in *The Friendship of Books* (London: Macmillan, 1893), p. 151.

3. Charles Kingsley, *Alton Locke,* chap. 30. I owe this reference to Dr. Lawrence Williams of the University of Dundee.

4. Sarah Austin to Barthélemy St. Hilaire, January 1862, in Janet Ross, *Three Generations of English Women* (London: T. F. Unwin, 1893), p. 385.

5. Published in F. A. Mignet, *Éloges Historiques* (Paris: Didier, 1864).

Chapter One

1. Pishey Thompson, *The History and Antiquities of Boston* (Boston: S. G. Drake, 1856), p. 456, n. Isaac Hallam's volume of poetry, *The Cocker,* was published in Stamford in 1742.

2. Alexander Carlyle, *Autobiography* (Edinburgh: W. Blackwood, 1860), pp. 280.

3. Mary Willett, *A History of West Bromwich* (West Bromwich: Free Press, 1882), p. 181.

4. Manuscript exercise book, Hallam papers, Christ Church; hereafter referred to as Ch.Ch.

5. See Charles Peers to Henry Hallam, 14 May 1795, Ch.Ch.

6. Register of undergraduates, li.b.3, Christ Church Archives, Oxford.

7. M. L. Clarke, *Greek Studies in England 1700–1830* (Cambridge: At the University Press, 1945), pp. 97–99.

8. Henry Cockburn, *Memorials of His Time* (Edinburgh: J. N. Foulis, 1909), p. 338.

9. Guendolen Ramsden, *Correspondence of Two Brothers* (London: Longmans Green, 1906), p. 98 and passim.

10. Add. MSS, d. 28, Trinity College, Cambridge, hereafter referred to as T.C.C.

11. Lord Webb Seymour to Henry Hallam, 9 May 1802, Ch.Ch.

12. Add. MSS, d. 28, T.C.C.

13. Add. MSS, d. 27, T.C.C.

14. Henry Hallam to Lord Webb Seymour, 27 May 1802, in Ramsden, p. 60

15. Henry Hallam to Elizabeth Hallam, 9 July 1802, Ch.Ch. See also Henry Hallam to Lord Mahon, 4 November 1847, Stanhope manuscripts, Chevening; hereafter referred to as Chevening.

16. See Add. MSS, d. 28, T.C.C.

17. Leonard Horner *Memoirs and Correspondence of Francis Horner M.P.* (London: John Murray, 1843), 1:178.

18. John Clive, *Scotch Reviewers* (London: Faber and Faber, 1957), p. 195.

19. Francis Jeffrey to Henry Hallam, 17 December 1804, Ch.Ch.

20. On Hallam's authorship of *Edinburgh Review* articles see Walter E. Houghton, *The Wellesley Index to Victorian Periodicals 1824–1900* (Toronto: At the University Press, 1966), 1:437, 438, 439, 443, 450, 488.

21. Lloyd Sanders *The Holland House Circle* (London: Methuen, 1908), pp. 224–25.

22. Francis Jeffrey to Henry Hallam, 21 February 1806; 6 May 1806, Ch.Ch.

23. Irwin Griggs et al., "Early Edinburgh Reviewers: A New List," *Modern Philology* 63 (February 1946): 200–201.

24. Francis Jeffrey to Henry Hallam, 27 November 1806, Ch.Ch.

25. Clive, pp. 108–10.

26. Francis Jeffrey to Henry Hallam, 7 June 1808; 20 August 1808, Ch.Ch.

27. Clive, pp. 111–12.

28. Francis Jeffrey to Henry Hallam, 9 December 1808. Ch.Ch.

29. Clive, pp. 114–15.

30. Francis Jeffrey to Henry Hallam, 6 October 1809, Ch.Ch.

31. See the doodles and irrelevant and irreverent verse amid notes on cases in Add. MSS, d.15, T.C.C.

32. *View of the State of Europe during the Middle Ages,* 2 vols. (London, 1818), 2:194.

33. Deduced from correspondence addressed to Hallam.

34. On Sir Abraham, see A[rthur] E[lton], *Clevedon Court* (London: National Trust, 1962), pp. 14–15.

35. *Middle Ages,* 2:499.

36. Culled from letters to Hallam over many years from his agents, Henry Rogers of Boston and Mrs. Ann Smith of West Bromwich, Ch.Ch.

37. Add. MSS, d.33; d.35, T.C.C.

38. Charles Abraham Elton to Henry Hallam, 28 December 1817, Ch.Ch.

39. Quoted in Lord Webb Seymour to Henry Hallam, 5 April 1812, Ch.Ch.

40. Lord Webb Seymour to Henry Hallam, 5 April 1812, Ch.Ch.

41. Henry Hallam to Lord Webb Seymour, 8 July 1813, in Ramsden, pp. 118–19.

42. Henry Hallam to John Murray, 22 November 1817, John Murray papers, London.

43. Henry Hallam to Lord Webb Seymour, 21 November 1818 and 23 December 1818, in Ramsden, pp. 247–54; Henry Hallam to John Murray, 7 July 1818, Murray papers. See also Arthur H. Hallam, *Remains* (London: John Murray, 1863), p. ix and J. R. Hale's introduction to *The Italian Journal*, by Samuel Rogers (London: Faber and Faber, 1957).

44. *Middle Ages*, 2:514.

45. Private information from Miss Elizabeth Lennard, a great granddaughter of Henry Hallam.

46. See letters from Francis Horner to Henry Hallam, Francis Horner papers, 1802–1816, British Library of Political and Economic Science, London School of Economics.

47. Henry Hallam to John Murray, 13 June 1825, Murray papers.

48. John P. Boileau, manuscript sketch of the life of Henry Hallam, Ch.Ch.

49. W. S. Rose, "Gundimore," in *Poems* (Brighton: Creasy and Baker, 1837), p. 84.

50. Henry Edward Fox, *Journal 1818–1830,* ed. earl of Ilchester (London, 1923), p. 153.

51. *Remains,* p. xi; Professor Schnell to Henry Hallam, 6 November 1822, Ch.Ch.; Peter Elmsley to Henry Hallam, 20 April 1822, Ch.Ch.

52. Henry Holland, *Recollection of Past Life* (London: Longmans Green, 1872), p. 226, n. See also William Sotheby to Henry Hallam, 26 August 1825, Ch.Ch.; Henry Hallam to Lord Mahon, 4 November 1856, Chevening.

53. *Middle Ages,* 11th ed. (London, 1855), 3:328, n.

54. T. H. Vail Motter, ed., *The Writings of Arthur Hallam,* (New York: Modern Language Association of America, 1943), pp. 4–5; Charles Milnes Gaskell, ed., *An Eton Boy* (London: Constable, 1939), pp. 120–58; Thomas Butt to Henry Hallam, 10 April 1804, Ch.Ch.

55. [Robert Southey] in *Quarterly Review* 37 (1828): 259–60.

56. Henry Hallam to John Murray, 3 January 1828, Murray papers.

57. Transcript of a letter from Henry Hallam to John Whishaw in the latter's handwriting, 10 March 1828, Murray papers.

58. John Whishaw to Henry Hallam, 3 April 1828, Ch.Ch.

59. Henry Hallam to John Whishaw, 28 April 1828, in Lady Seymour, *The "Pope" of Holland House* (London: T. F. Unwin, 1906), pp. 319–22.

60. John Murray to Henry Hallam, 27 May 1828, Ch.Ch.

61. John Whishaw to Henry Hallam, 2 February 1828, Ch.Ch.

62. Lord Cockburn, quoted in George Otto Trevelyan *Life and Letters of Lord Macaulay* (London: Longmans Green, 1876), 1:139.

63. John Whishaw to Henry Hallam, 3 April 1828, Ch.Ch.

64. [T. B. Macaulay], "Hallam's *Constitutional History of England*," *Edinburgh Review* 48 (1828):96–169; reprinted in Lord Macaulay, *Critical and Historical Essays* (London: Everyman, 1907), 1:1–76.

65. Macaulay, 1:4, 11, 21.

66. H. Hale Bellot, *University College London 1826–1926* (London: At the University Press, 1929), pp. 29, 37.

67. Cf. George Ticknor, *Life, Journal and Letters* (London: Sampson Low, 1876), 2:148: (30 March 1838) "Among other things, I asked him [Hallam] about the universities, knowing that his relations to them are somewhat peculiar, as he was educated at Oxford, and sent his son to Cambridge, where he much distinguished himself at Trinity. His replies were such as I anticipated, very cold as far as concerns Oxford, on which he has thus decidedly turned his back, but less favourable to either than I supposed they would be."

68. Henry Hallam to Leonard Horner, 9 July 1831, University College of London papers (hereafter, U.C.L. papers), University College Library, London.

69. Bellot, p. 204.

70. Henry Hallam to Leonard Horner, 9 July 1831, U.C.L. papers, University College Library, London.

71. Henry Hallam to Leonard Horner, 17 October 1831, in Katherine M. Lyell *Memoir of Leonard Horner* (London: Women's Printing Society, 1890), 1:257–92.

72. Chester W. New, *The Life of Henry Brougham to 1830* (Oxford: Clarendon Press, 1961), p. 350.

73. Henry Hallam to Thomas Coates, 28 April 1833, Society for the Diffusion of Useful Knowledge papers (hereafter, S.D.U.K. papers), University College Library, London.

74. Henry Hallam to the S.D.U.K., May 1836, S.D.U.K. papers, University College Library, London.

75. Henry Hallam to Lord Mahon, 2 October 1835, Chevening.

76. F. A. Mignet, *Eloges Historiques* (Paris, 1864), p. 301.

77. Charles Tennyson, *Tennyson* (London: Macmillan, 1949), pp. 87, 112, 117. See also Motter, passim.

78. See Frances Brookfield, *The Cambridge Apostles* (London: I. Pitman, 1906), passim.

79. Alfred Tennyson, *In Memoriam,* xix.

80. Henry Hallam to Alfred Tennyson, 10 October 1833, Tennyson papers, Tennyson Research Centre, Lincoln.

81. Charles Tennyson, p. 50.

82. Jane Elton To W. H. Brookfield, 7 October 1841, in Charles Brookfield et al., *Mrs. Brookfield and Her Circle* (London: I. Pitman, 1905), 1:102.

83. Henry Hallam to Alfred Tennyson, 6 February 1834, Tennyson papers, Tennyson Research Centre, Lincoln.

84. Henry Hallam to John Murray, 10 December 1835, Murray papers, London.

85. Henry Hallam to John Murray, 24 February 1837, Murray papers, London.

86. On one occasion a visitor to Hallam's London house was surprised to see "a large swarthy man arise from the hearthrug where he had been lying at full length and advance with outstretched hand, saying in a deep voice: 'I am Septimus, the most morbid of the Tennysons' " (Charles Tennyson, p. 199).

87. Hallam to Sir Robert Peel, 11 February 1845, Peel papers, add. MSS, 40559.310, British Library.

88. Sir Robert Peel to Henry Hallam, 15 February 1845, Ch.Ch.

89. W. M. Thackeray to Mrs. Brookfield, 2 January 1849, in W. M. Thackeray, *Letters and Private Papers,* ed. G. N. Ray (Oxford: Clarendon Press, 1945), 2:492.

90. For fuller discussion see D. S. L. Cardwell, *The Organisation of Science in England* (London: Heinemann, 1957). See also G. Kitson Clark, *The Making of Victorian England* (London: Methuen, 1962), pp. 260–62.

91. Henry Hallam to Charles Babbage, n.d., Babbage papers, add. MSS, 37188.126 and add Mss, 37188.551, British Library.

92. *Annals of the Royal Statistical Society 1834–1934* (London, 1934), pp. 22, 89.

93. *Gentleman's Magazine,* n.s. 5 (March 1836):292; Joan Evans, *A History of the Society of Antiquaries* (Oxford: At the University Press, 1956), p. 242; Arundell Esdaile, *The British Museum Library* (London: Allen and Unwin, 1946), p. 324.

94. William Jerdan, *Men I Have Known* (London: G. Routledge, 1866) pp. 246–47.

95. *Gentleman's Magazine,* n.s. 5 (August 1836): 187.

96. W. Jerdan to Henry Hallam, 8 February 1848, Ch.Ch.; John Foster, *Alumni Oxonienses 1715–1886* (London: Parker and Co., 1888), *sub* Hallam.

97. Foster.

98. Henry Hallam to Lord Mahon, 9 September 1842, Chevening.

99. Edward Everett to Henry Hallam, 19 September 1848, Ch.Ch.

100. Henry Hallam to Sir Robert Peel, 7 March 1846, Peel papers, Add. MSS. 42586.206, British Library.

101. Lord Carlisle's Journal, quoted in Trevelyan, 2:192.

102. A. F. Rio, quoted and translated by David Alec Wilson, *Carlyle on Cromwell and Others* (London: Kegan Paul, 1925), p. 55.

103. Everett's journal, quoted in P. R. Frothingham, *Edward Everett* (Boston: Houghton Mifflin, 1925), pp. 195–6.

104. Frothingham, p. 38.

105. F. Guizot to Henry Hallam, 14 March 1838, Ch.Ch.

106. Pierre M. Irving, *Life and Letters of Washington Irving,* 4 vols. (London: Bohn, 1862), 1:386.

107. See Henry Hallam to W. H. Prescott, 1 June 1838, in Roger Wolcott, ed., *Correspondence of William Hickling Prescott 1833–1845* (Boston: Houghton Mifflin, 1925), pp. 35–36.

108. "Mr. Webster approaches as nearly to the *beau ideal* of a Republican Senator as any man that I have ever seen in the course of my life; worthy of Rome or Venice, rather than of our noisy and wrangling generation" (Henry Hallam to Mrs. Ticknor, in G. T. Curtis, *Life of Daniel Webster* [New York; D. Appleton, 1870], 2:27).

109. Edward Everett to Henry Hallam, 13 August 1845, Ch.Ch.

110. Henry Hallam to Edward Everett, 15 November 1845, Everett papers, Massachusetts Historical Society Library, Boston, Massachusetts; hereafter referred to as M.H.S.

111. Charles Brookfield et al., *Mrs. Brookfield and Her Circle* (London: I. Pitman, 1905), 1:103.; Henry Hallam to Lord Mahon, 31 August 1842, Chevening.; Francis Galton, *Memories of My Life* (London: Methuen, 1908), p. 79; Charles Brookfield, 1:182.

112. George Bancroft to W. H. Prescott, 3 March 1847, in Wolcott, p. 625.

113. Henry Hallam to John Murray, 24 November 1845, Murray papers, London.

114. Henry Hallam to Edward Everett, 9 March 1848, Everett papers, M.H.S.

115. "It is not a *new* work as I wish to have it understood" (Henry Hallam to John Murray, n.d., Murray papers, London).

116. Henry Hallam to Lord Mahon, 30 August 1848, Chevening.

117. Henry Hallam to Lady Mahon, n.d., Chevening.

118. Henry Hallam to Edward Everett, 23 March 1849, Everett papers, M.H.S.

119. Henry Hallam to W. E. Gladstone, 6 April 1840, Add MSS, 44375.108; 2 April 1846, Add MSS, 44364.4, Gladstone Papers, British Library.

120. H. S. M[aine] et al., *Memoir of Henry Fitzmaurice Hallam* (n.d.), p. 11; Henry Hallam to Lord Mahon, 6 October 1850, Chevening.

121. Henry Hallam to Samuel Rogers, 26 November 1850, in P. W. Clayden, *Rogers and His Contemporaries* (London: Smith, Elder and Co., 1889), 2:379.

122. John Morley, *Life of W. E. Gladstone* (London: Macmillan, 1905), 1:290.

123. Macaulay's journal, 2 November 1850, in Trevelyan, 2:288.

124. W. M. Thackeray to Mrs. June Brookfield, 23 December 1850, in Thackeray, 2:714.

125. Henry Hallam to John Murray, 2 December 1851, Murray papers, London.

126. Henry Hallam to Lord Mahon, 6 October 1851; 8 September 1851, Chevening.

127. Henry Hallam to W. H. Prescott, 24 March 1853, Prescott papers, M.H.S.

128. Henry Hallam to Lord Mahon, 22 December 1851, Chevening.

129. Henry Hallam to George Bancroft (typed copy), 11 March 1852, Bancroft papers, M.H.S.

130. George Bancroft to Henry Hallam, 10 February 1852, Ch.Ch.

131. Henry Hallam to John Murray, 13 January 1854, Murray papers; Henry Holland, p. 226.

132. Macaulay's journal, 13 February 1856, in Trevelyan, 2:396.

133. Holland, pp. 226–27.

134. Henry Hallam to Sir Arthur Elton, 29 June 1854, Elton papers, Clevedon Court, Somerset.

135. "I return you Mme Sand's novel, which is not, I think, much above mediocrity" (Henry Hallam to Lord Mahon, 1 April 1854, Chevening).

136. Hoare & Co. Bankers receipt, Ch.Ch. Another elderly historian who more improbably dabbled in railway stock was John Lingard. See Martin Haile et al., *Life and Letters of John Lingard* (London: Herbert and Daniel, [1911]), p. 289.

137. Henry Hallam to Lord Mahon, 13 January 1854, Chevening; Henry Hallam to W. H. Prescott, 8 December 1855, in George Ticknor,

Life of W. H. Prescott (London: Routledge, Warne and Routledge, 1864), p. 444; Henry Hallam to Lady Stanhope, 6 June 1855, Chevening; receipt for purchase of books, Ch.Ch.

138. J. L. Motley to Mrs. Motley, 6 June 1858, in J. L. Motley *Correspondence*, ed. G. W. Curtis (London: John Murray, 1889), 1:251.

139. J. Farnaby Cator to Earl Stanhope, 16 January 1859, Chevening; J. Farnaby Cator to Earl Stanhope, 21 January 1859, Chevening.

Chapter Two

1. Henry Hallam to Lord Webb Seymour, 5 November 1813, in Guendolen Ramsden, *Correspondence of Two Brothers* (London: Longmans Green, 1906), pp. 123–25; *Middle Ages,* 11th ed., 1:386, n., 460, n.

2. See Lord Webb Seymour to Henry Hallam, 5 April 1812, Ch.Ch.; *Middle Ages,* 11th ed., 3:159n.

3. Henry Hallam to Lord Webb Seymour, 8 July 1813, in Ramsden, pp. 117–20.

4. See *Middle Ages,* 11th ed., 3:369, n., 428, n.; 2:262, n.

5. Trinity College Library, Add. MSS, d. 28.

6. *Middle Ages,* 1:500n; 2:576.

7. A. H. Huth, *Life and Writings of Henry Thomas Buckle* (London: Sampson Low, 1880), 1:13.

8. Henry Hallam to Lord Mahon, 19 October 1837, Chevening. On German historical scholarship of the time, and its influence in Britain see Klaus Dockhorn, *Der Deutsche Historismus in England,* (Göttingen: Vandenhoeck and Ruprecht, 1950) and D. Forbes, *"Historismus* in England" *Cambridge Journal* 4 (1951):387–400.

9. Thomas Arnold, *Lectures in Modern History* (London, 1845), p. 27.

10. Caroline Fox, *Memories of Old Friends,* ed. H. N. Pym (London, 1882), 2:136–39.

11. Southey was "a gentleman, who is distinguished among many other talents, for an unrivalled felicity in expressing the peculiar manner of authors whom he translates or imitates" (*Middle Ages,* 2:592, n.)

12. See Francis Horner to Henry Hallam, in Leonard Horner, ed., *Memoir of Francis Horner, M.P.* (London: John Murray, 1843), 1:428–30.

13. *Middle Ages,* 2:416; 1:ix; 2:418; 1:333, 505.

14. *Edinburgh Review* 12, no. 23 (1808): 188.

15. *Middle Ages,* 2:416–17; 1:ix, 435; 2:513; 1:31.

16. *Edinburgh Review* 6, no. 11 (1805):214.

17. *Middle Ages,* 1:39; 11th ed., 2:1; 1:4–5; 2:455.

18. Ibid., 2:436, 438, 611, n., 437, 421; 1:31; 2:154, 3; 1:31; 2:442–43.

19. J. J. Saunders, *Aspects of the Crusades* (Christchurch, New Zealand: University of Canterbury Press, 1962), pp. 12, 14. Similarly, the French Mandate in Syria gave a boost to Crusader studies in France.

20. I use the word "historicism" as the English translation of the German, *Historismus*. See Forbes, "Historismus in England." This is essentially a review of Dockhorn, *Der Deutsche Historismus in England.*

21. Hallam's discussion of the Crusades is in *Middle Ages*, 2:32–40.

22. *Edinburgh Review* 7, no. 13 (1805):94.

23. *Middle Ages*, 2:8.

24. See T. L. Coonan, "John Lingard" in *Some Modern Historians of Britain*, ed. Herman Ausubel (New York: Dryden Press, 1951), p. 7.

25. *Middle Ages*, 1:31.

26. Ibid., 2:2; 1:235; 2:53; 1:269; 2:31, 57–58, 89, 63, 92.

27. Ibid., 2:35, 105, 101.

28. Ibid., 1:263; 2:437, 505.

29. Ibid., 2:120.

30. On Lingard see in addition to the article by Coonan; P. Hughes, "John Lingard," *History Today*, April 1951, pp. 57–62; and Martin Haile et al., *Life and Letters of John Lingard* (London: Herbert and Daniel, [1911]).

31. "What was the principal adversary of this tremendous power? By whom was it checked, and resisted, and put down? By none, and by nothing, but the direct and manifest interposition of God" (Arnold, p. 139).

32. *Middle Ages*, 1:389; 2:94; 1:254.

33. A. Momigliano, "Gibbon's Contribution to Historical Method," in *Studies in Historiography* (London: Weidenfeld and Nicolson, 1966), p. 52.

34. *Middle Ages*, 2:446–47, 125, 124.

35. Ibid., 2:127.

36. See C. Hill, "The Norman Yoke" in *Democracy and the Labour Movement*, ed. John Saville (London: Lawrence and Wishart, 1954), pp. 11–66; R. T. Vann, "The Free Anglo-Saxons: A Historical Myth," *Journal of the History of Ideas* 19 (1958): 259–72.

37. David Hume, *History of England* (London: Longmans Green, 1854), 1:162.

38. See Hill; David C. Douglas, *The Norman Conquest and British Historians* (Glasgow: Jackson, 1946); Asa Briggs, *Saxons, Normans and Victorians* (London: Historical Association, 1966).

39. Helen Cam in *Historical Novels* (London: Historical Association, 1961), p. 8., says that "Lytton's Harold is a high-principled statesman of the early 19th century."

40. J. G. A. Pocock, "Robert Brady 1627–1700," *Cambridge Historical Journal* 10 (1951):194–95.

41. Hume, 1:448, 221.

42. *Middle Ages,* 2:162, n.

43. Ibid., 2:159, 161, 166, 167.

44. Ibid., 1:140; 2:174, n.

45. Ibid., 2:177–78.

46. Hume, 1:494.

47. John Millar, *An Historical View of the English Constitution* (London: Stranan and Cadell, 1787), 1:298.

48. *Middle Ages,* 2:177, 178; Stubbs, 1:558, 571, 572.

49. John Richard Green, *A Short History of the English People* (London, 1891), p. 50; and on the historiography of Magna Carta, see A. Pallister, "Magna Carta: Its Influence on Politics and Political Thought Since 1600" (Ph. D. thesis, University of Nottingham, 1966), chaps. 3–4.

50. *Middle Ages,* 2:181.

51. Ibid., 2:195.

52. Ibid., 2:199.

53. For the next few paragraphs I have received help and guidance from the following articles, pamphlets, and books: H. Cam, "Stubbs Seventy Years After," in *Cambridge Historical Journal,* vol. 9 (Cambridge, 1948), pp. 129–47; J. G. Edwards, *William Stubbs* (London; Historical Association, 1952), and *Historians and the Medieval English Parliament* (Glasgow, 1960); C. H. Knowles, *Simon de Montfort 1265–1965* (London: Historical Association, 1965); M. McKisack, "Edward III and the Historians," *History* 45 (February 1960):1–15; Edward Miller, *The Origins of Parliament* (London: Historical Association, 1960); J. G. A. Pocock, "Robert Brady 1627–1700," *Cambridge Historical Journal* 10 (1951):186–204, and *The Ancient Constitution and the Feudal Law* (Cambridge: At the University Press, 1957), pp. 182–228; G. Templeman, "Edward I and the Historians," *Cambridge Historical Journal* 10 (1950):16–35.

54. Pocock, *Ancient Constitution,* p. 266.

55. David C. Douglas, *English Scholars 1660–1730* (London: Eyre Spottiswood, 1951), p. 125.

56. *Middle Ages,* 2:236, 237, 162, n., 224, 225, n.

57. Ibid., 2:247.

58. Hume, 2:314, 324.

59. Thomas Carte, *History of England* (London, privately published, 1747–55), 2:540.

60. Hume, 2:290.

61. *Middle Ages,* 2:275.

62. Hume, 2:291–92.

63. Carte, 2:518.

64. *Middle Ages,* 2:276, 278.

65. Ibid., 2:282, 283–84.

66. Hume, 2:304, 324.

67. *Middle Ages,* 2:286, n.

68. As suggested by Professor Trevor-Roper. See H. Trevor-Roper, "David Hume," *The Listener,* 7 October 1965, pp. 521–24.

69. Bertrand Russell, *History of Western Philosophy* (London: Allen and Unwin, 1946), p. 686.

70. *Middle Ages,* 2:355, 414.

71. Ibid., 2:361, 362.

72. Ibid., 2:302.

73. Ibid., 2:316.

74. Ibid., 2:367–68.

75. Ibid., 2:367. It is interesting to note that Hallam speaks of "Mr" Hume as a contemporary and of the state of "our" liberties as possessed equally by Hume and himself. Hume's volumes on the Middle Ages were published in 1761 and he died the year before Hallam was born.

76. *Middle Ages,* 2:414.

Chapter Three

1. By, for example, H. Trevor-Roper, "Macaulay," *The Listener,* 14 October 1965, p. 566. Professor Trevor-Roper confuses Henry and Arthur Hallam.

2. This has been discussed by D. Forbes in his introduction *History of England,* by David Hume (Harmondsworth: Penguin, 1970).

3. See W. H. Lehmann, *John Millar of Glasgow* (Cambridge: At the University Press, 1960), pp. 145–63.

4. D. H. Pennington, "Cromwell and the Historians," *History Today* 8 (September 1958):601.

5. The next five paragraphs owe much to the following: J. Anderson, "Sir Walter Scott and History" (Ph.D. thesis, University of Edinburgh, 1965), pp. 85–142; L. M. Donnelly, "The Celebrated Mrs. Macaulay," *William and Mary Quarterly* 6 (April 1949):173–204; C. H. Firth, "The Development of the Study of 17th century History," *Transactions of the Royal Historical Society* 7 (1913):25–48; D. B. Horn, "Some Scottish Writers of History in the 18th Century," *Scottish Historical Review* 40 (January 1961):1–18; T. P. Peardon, *The Transition in English Historical Writing 1760–1830* (New York: Columbia University Press, 1933), pp. 69–102, 183–213.

6. Reprinted in Lord Macaulay, *Critical and Historical Essays* (London: Everyman, 1907), 1:174–75.

7. *Constitutional History of England from the Accession of Henry VII to the Death of George II,* 2 vols. (London, 1827), 1:1–2, 11.

8. David Hume, *History of England,* 3:8, 63, 141, 253, 255, 298, 365, 379.

9. *Constitutional History,* 1:37, 47, 48. The poet, Thomas Moore, was fascinated by Hallam's use of the archaic word "imped." See Thomas Moore, *Memoirs, Journal and Correspondence,* ed. Lord J. Russell (London: Longmans Green, 1853–56), 5:222.

10. Ibid., 1:49–50, 51.

11. Ibid., 1:34, n., 113, n., 45, n., 77, n., 90, n., 95. However, he also writes elsewhere: "Collier, though with many prejudices of his own, is, all things considered, the fairest of our ecclesiastical writers as to this reign" (ibid., 1:74, n.).

12. Ibid., 1:172.

13. Ibid., 1:76, 77, 78, 86, 85.

14. Ibid., 1:81–82.

15. Ibid., 1:84.

16. Ibid., 1:101

17. Hume, 4:351.

18. *Constitutional History,* 1:305.

19. *Middle Ages,* 2:365, n.

20. Hume, 4:351, 501, quoting from Walter Raleigh, *History of the World*; and *Constitutional History,* 1:298–300.

21. Ibid., 4:349, 355, 356–57, 359, 361. A twentieth-century Tory historian, Sir Keith Feiling, also invokes Shakespeare—along with other great minds of the age, Bacon, Hooker, Hobbes—as being enlisted on the side of authority. See K. G. Feiling, *England Under the Tudors and Stuarts* (Oxford: At the University Press, 1945), p. 129.

22. *Constitutional History,* 1:181, 265, 284, 254.

23. Ibid., 1:254.

24. Ibid., 1:251, 258, 261.

25. Ibid., 1:298–99, 273, 303, 230, 305, 303.

26. Ibid., 1:306.

27. Ibid., 1:284.

28. See E. M. W. Tillyard, *The Elizabethan World Picture* (Harmondsworth: Penguin, 1963), pp. 18–20.

29. *Constitutional History,* 1:306, 223, 248, 306.

30. Robert Southey, *The Book of the Church* (London: John Murray, 1848), p. 419.

31. Hume, 5:126.

32. J. B. Mozley, *Essays Historical and Theological* (London: Rivingtons, 1878), 1:227.

33. See C. H. Simpkinson, *The Life and Times of William Laud* (London: John Murray, 1894), p. iii: "The strange misrepresentations of the career and

character of William Laud . . . are mainly to be attributed to the fierce invective of Macaulay and the cold criticism of Hallam."

34. *Constitutional History,* 1:433–34, 519, 516, 427, 522, 494–95, 501.

35. Ibid., 1:541, 432, 170, 435.

36. Ibid., 1:417, 418, 464, 460, 501, 509.

37. Ibid., 1:592, 474–75, 546–47.

38. Ibid., 1:567, 562–63.

39. Ibid., 1:563, 588–89.

40. Ibid., 1:602–5, 573.

41. Ibid., 1:615.

42. Ibid., 2:298, 115, 116, 125; 1:91; 2:129, n., 131.

43. Ibid., 2:152, 135.

44. Ibid., 2:251, 325.

45. On the historiography of 1688, see J. G. A. Pocock, *The Ancient Constitution and the Feudal Law,* pp. 229–51; M. Ashley, "King James II and the Revolution of 1688: Some Reflections on the Historiography," in *Historical Essays 1600–1750,* ed. H. E. Bell (London: A. and C. Black, 1963), pp. 185–202.

46. *Constitutional History,* 2:447, 407, 444.

47. Ibid., 2:435, 448, 449, 550.

48. Ibid., 2:331, 551, 273, 562.

49. Lord Macaulay, *Miscellaneous Writings* (London: Longmans Green, 1880), 3:99–100.

50. H. Butterfield, *The Whig Interpretation of History* (London, 1929), passim.

51. *Constitutional History,* 2:325. In later editions Hallam omitted the rather cynical words from, "the proverbial saying. . . ."

52. Ibid., 2:218–19, 277, 537.

53. Henry Hallam to Lord Mahon, 2 October 1835, and 14 September 1836, in Chevening.

Chapter Four

1. *Introduction to the Literature of Europe during the Fifteenth, Sixteenth and Seventeenth Centuries,* 4 vols (London, 1837–39), 4:607.

2. René Wellek, *The Rise of English Literary History* (Chapel Hill: University of North Carolina Press, 1941): 201.

3. *Literature of Europe,* 1:xvi.

4. W. F. Monypenny et al., *The Life of Benjamin Disraeli,* 2 vols. (London: John Murray, 1929), 1:469–70.

5. George Saintsbury, A. W. Ward, Oliver Elton, and René Wellek all

speak highly of the work. Professor L. W. Forster of the University of Cambridge tells me that he recommends the work to his students of European literature.

6. According to Sir Henry Holland, Hallam discussed this problem with his doctor. "The scheme of such a History, perhaps too large in itself, involved the necessity of choice among three methods, based severally on the division of time, of country, and of literary subject—all important, but each method more or less excluding the other two. Hallam more than once came to talk with me on the question before he began to write. The difficulty just stated was fully felt and discussed" (Henry Holland, *Recollections of Past Life* [London: Longmans Green, 1872], p. 227, n.).

7. Henry Hallam to John Murray, 10 December 1835, Murray papers, London.

8. *Literature of Europe,* 1:420.

9. Ibid., 3:136.

10. Ibid., 2:85; 4:122–23; 1:405, n.; 4:444; 3:62, n.; 4:322, 274; 3:386, 448.

11. Ibid., 2:73, 482; 1:xv–xvi.

12. Ibid., 1:157; 2:133, n.

13. Ibid., 1:155, 642.

14. Ibid., 1:530; 2:164.

15. Ibid., 1:563, 303–4; 3:166.

16. Ibid., 3:227, 168, n., 228.

17. Ibid., 4:564.

18. Ibid., 3:515; 1:222.

19. Ibid., 1:443, 445, 448, 625; 3:492, 24, 25; 1:13; 2:322; 3:652, 469; 2:40, 363.

20. Ibid., 2:326, 313, 333, 324, 334.

21. It was told, and documented, in A. H. Nethercot, "The Reputation of the 'Metaphysical Poets' during the Age of Johnson and the Romantic Revival," *Studies in Philology* 22 (1929):81–132.

22. *Literature of Europe,* 3:492, 473, 493.

23. Quoted in George Watson, *The Literary Critics* (Harmondsworth: Penguin, 1963), pp. 138–39.

24. *Literature of Europe,* 3:504.

25. On Hallam as Shakespearian critic, see Augustus Ralli, *A History of Shakespearian Criticism* (Oxford: At the University Press, 1932), 1:188–90.

26. *Literature of Europe,* 2:386, 388, 396–97; 3:564, 566, 394–95.

27. Ibid., 3:574, 575, 576, 579–81.

28. Samuel Johnson, *Lives of the Poets* (London: Everyman, 1961), 1:96.

29. *Literature of Europe,* 3:514.

30. Samuel Taylor Coleridge, *Biographia Literaria* (London: Everyman, 1962, pp. 168–69.

31. Quoted in J. Huizinga, *Men and Ideas*, trans. J. S. Holmes (London: Eyre Spottiswood, 1960), p. 256. For this paragraph, see also Wallace K. Ferguson, *The Renaissance in Historical Thought* (Boston: Houghton Mifflin, 1948); J. R. Hale, *England and The Italian Renaissance* (London: Grey Arrow, 1963); H. Weisinger, "The English Origins of the Sociological Interpretation of the Renaissance," *Journal of the History of Ideas* 11 (1950):321–38, and "English Attitudes Towards the Relationship between the Renaissance and Reformation," *Church History* 14 (1945): 167–87. In the last two essays, the term "English" is extended to mean also "Scottish."

32. *Literature of Europe,* 1:83, 97–98, 173.

33. Ibid., 1:141, 143.

34. Ibid., 1:197.

35. Ibid., 1:411, 406, 414, 418, 513–14.

36. Ibid., 1:358; 2:31.

37. This paragraph implicitly takes issue with views put forward by Sir Herbert Butterfield in *The Whig Interpretation of History.* Sir Herbert mentions no names in his criticisms of the "Whig" view of Luther and the Reformation—that it *was* a stage in the rise of liberty. However, one of the few "Whig" historians to whom he refers in the book is Hallam. It might be inferred that Hallam held this "Whig" view. As I have already mentioned, Hallam is elsewhere guilty of the "Whiggism" criticized by Professor Butterfield.

38. *Literature of Europe,* 1:485, 521; 2:111, 112.

39. Ibid., 2:414, 1, 497–99; 2:94.

40. Ibid., 1:511; 2:95; 3:321; 4:135.

41. Ibid., 3:102, 117.

42. O. Elton, in *Prefaces and Essays,* by George Saintsbury (London, 1945), p. 2.

43. Benjamin Disraeli noticed this during his honeymoon reading. "In general, I see a dash of German affectation in his style, which he has imbibed of late" (Benjamin Disraeli to Sarah Disraeli, 2 October 1839, in Monypenny, 1:470).

44. *Literature of Europe,* 2:457, 439.

Chapter Five

1. Add. MSS. d.28, Trinity College Cambridge.

2. Cf. C. R. Fay, *Adam Smith and the Scotland of His Day* (Cambridge: At the University Press, 1956), p. 85: "Even in 1800 political economy needed some sponsoring."

3. On this period of English historical scholarhsip, see D. C. Douglas, "The Development of English Medieval Scholarship 1660–1730," *Transac-*

tions of the Royal Historical Society 21 (1939):21–39, and *English Scholars 1660–1730*.

4. Quoted by Joan Evans in *A History of the Society of Antiquaries* (Oxford: At the University Press, 1956), p. 146.

5. Quoted by H. R. Trevor-Roper in "Edward Gibbon after 200 Years," *The Listener,* 22 October 1964, p. 619.

6. Laurence Eachard, quoted by D. W. L. Earl, "Paul Rapin de Thoyras" (M.Litt. thesis, Cambridge University, 1961), p. 81.

7. A point made by R. N. Stromberg, "History in the 18th Century," *Journal of the History of Ideas* 12 (1951):295–304. See also A. Skinner, "Economics and History: the Scottish Enlightenment," *Scottish Journal of Political Economy* 12 (February 1965):1–22; D. Forbes, "Scientific Whiggism: Adam Smith and John Millar," *Cambridge Journal* 7 (August 1954):643–70.

8. Quoted in Douglas, "The Development of English Medieval Scholarship," p. 380.

9. Sir John Clerk to Roger Gale, 1736, quoted in Evans, p. 99.

10. James Boswell, *Life of Samuel Johnson* (London: Everyman, 1907), 1:559, 470.

11. Quoted in T. P. Peardon, *The Transition of English Historical Writing 1760–1830* (New York: Columbia University Press, 1933), pp. 133, 247, 138.

12. Quoted in Martin Hale et al., *Life and Letters of John Lingard* (London: Herbert and Daniel, [1911]), p. 95.

13. *Constitutional History,* 1:79. Cf. John Webster, *The Duchess of Malfi,* act 5, scene 3 lines 10–18:

> I do love these ancient ruins,
> We never tread upon them but we set
> Our foot upon some reverend history:
> And, questionless, here in this open court,
> Which now lies naked to the injuries
> Of stormy weather, Some men lie interr'd
> Lov'd the church so well, and gave so largely to't,
> They thought it should have canopied their bones
> Till domesday; but all things have their end.

14. See W. S. Lewis, "Horace Walpole, Antiquary," in *Essays Presented to Sir Lewis Namier,* ed. Richard Pares (London: Macmillan, 1956), pp. 178–203.

15. Walter Scott, "Walpole," in *Lives of the Novelists* (Oxford: At the University Press, 1906), p. 191.

16. Scott,   "Mrs.   Radcliffe,"   in   ibid.,   pp.   327–28.

17. On the opening up of the public records, see Peardon, pp. 284–310. Scotland had a better record in the care of public records. See H. M. Paton, "The General Register House," *Book of the Old Edinburgh Club* 17 (1930):147–75.

18. Quoted by P. Hughes in "John Lingard," *History Today* 1 (April 1951):59.

19. Quoted in Haile, p. 138.

20. *Report of the Selected Committee of the House of Commons on the Records Commission,* quoted in Peardon, pp. 306–7.

21. Henry Hallam and R. H. Inglis, *Survey of the Principal Repositories of the Public Records* (London, 1833).

22. *Report . . . on the Records Commission* (1836), par. 7636.

23. F. J. Levy, "The Founding of the Camden Society," *Victorian Studies* 7 (March 1964):295–305.

24. For which, see David Knowles, *Great Historical Enterprises* (London: Nelson, 1963), pp. 101–34. See also D. M. Stenton, "The Pipe Rolls and the Historians 1600–1883," *Cambridge Historical Journal* 10 (July 1952):271–82.

25. On history at Oxford, see Charles Oman, *On the Writing of History* (London: Methuen, 1939), pp. 221–60; and at Cambridge, J. O. McLachlan, "The Origin and Early Development of the Cambridge Historical Tripos," *Cambridge Historical Journal* 9 (July 1947):78–98.

26. This has been discussed by Sir Llewellyn Woodward, in "The Rise of the Professional Historian," in *Studies in International History,* ed. K. Bourne and D. C. Watt (London: Longmans, 1967), pp. 16–34.

27. R. A. L. Smith, "Hallam's History," in *Collected Papers* (London: Longmans, 1947), p. 117.

Selected Bibliography

PRIMARY SOURCES

1. Published Works
During Hallam's lifetime, there were eleven editions of the *Middle Ages*, the editions published after 1848 incorporating the *Supplemental Notes*. A version, edited by William Smith, appeared in 1871 as *The Student's Middle Ages*, and the chapter on the English constitution was published together with De Lolme's *On the English Constitution* in 1870. There were editions of the whole work in 1868 and 1872. In the United States the work had greater success and at least four editions were published there in the 1880s and 1890s. There were, apart from two pirated editions in Paris, four editions of a French translation. An Italian edition was published in Florence in 1874.

The *Constitutional History* had more staying power. There were eleven editions up to 1866. William Smith produced a *Student's Constitutional History* in 1872 and G. Parker a digest called *Analysis of Hallam's Constitutional History* in 1879, reprinted in 1886. John Murray produced their last edition in 1901 and J. H. Morgan introduced an edition in 1912 for the Everyman library, which was published again in 1930. In the United States there were two separate editions with different introductions in the 1890s. Guizot supervised a French translation in 1832 and a French précis of the work also appeared. The *Constitutional History* is the only one of Hallam's works to be translated into German. It appeared as *Die Geschichte der Verfassung von England von Heinrich VII bis Georg II* in Leipzig in 1828—not only a speedy translation but also with an additional extra, a continuation of the history from 1760 to 1828.

The *Literature of Europe* went through five editions in Hallam's lifetime, and four afterward, the last in 1882. It has fared poorly in the United States with only three editions. There was, soon after it was first published, a French translation. The *Literary Essays and Characters,* extracts from the work, which was published in 1852, was never reissued.

"Ranken's *History of France.*" *Edinburgh Review* 6 (1805):209–28.
"Hints Respecting the Education of a Young Princess." *Edinburgh Review* 7 (1805):91–100.

"Inquiry into the Principles of Taste." Edinburgh Review 7 (1806):295–328.

"Throckmorton on the Catholic Question." *Edinburgh Review* 8 (1806):311–26.

"Gillies's *History of the World."* Edinburgh Review 11 (1807):40–61.

"History of the House of Austria." Edinburgh Review 12 (1808):181–202.

"Scott's Edition of John Dryden." *Edinburgh Review* 13 (1808):116–35.

"Johnes's translation of Joinville." *Edinburgh Review* 13 (1809):469–77.

"Elton's translation of Hesiod." *Edinburgh Review* 15 (1809):109–18.

"Elton's *Translations from the Classic Poets."* Quarterly Review 13 (1815):151–58.

View of the State of Europe during the Middle Ages, 2 vols. London: John Murray, 1818.

Constitutional History of England from the Accession of Henry VII to the Death of George II. 2 vols. London: John Murray, 1827.

"Lingard's *History of England."* Edinburgh Review 53 (1831):1–43.

"Palgrave's *Rise of the English Commonwealth."* Edinburgh Review 55 (1832):305–37.

Survey of the Principal Repositories of the Public Records, London, 1833. With Sir R. H. Inglis.

Remains in Verse and Prose of Arthur Henry Hallam. Edited by Arthur Hallam. Privately printed, 1834. Reprint. London: John Murray, 1864.

Introduction to the Literature of Europe during the Fifteenth, Sixteenth and Seventeenth Centuries. 4 vols. London: John Murray, 1837–39. Volumes 2–4 appeared in 1839.

"Memoir of Lord Webb Seymour." In *Memoir and Correspondence of Francis Horner, M. P.,* edited by Leonard Horner. London, 1843. 1:533–46.

[A letter to the editor, making detailed criticisms of a report on the Irish census]. *Journal of the Statistical Society* 7 (1844):178–80.

[A letter to the editor on a philological point about Rinuccini]. *Transactions of the Royal Society of Literature,* 2d ser. 2 (1844):50–58.

"On the Anglo Saxon Kings denominated Bretwaldas." *Archaeologia* 32 (1847):245–54.

Supplemental Notes to the View of the State of Europe during the Middle Ages. London: John Murray, 1848.

"Observations on the story of Lucius, the first Christian King of Britain." *Archaeologia* 33 (1849):308–25.

"On the chances of Hannibal at the Beginning of the Second Punic War." *Transactions of the Royal Society of Literature,* 2d ser. 4 (1850):109–14.

Literary Essays and Characters. London: John Murray, 1852.

2. Manuscript Sources

Boston. Massachusetts Historical Society. Everett papers; Ticknor papers; Prescott papers.

Cambridge. Trinity College Library. Hallam papers.

Chevening, Kent. Stanhope papers.

London. British Library. Gladstone papers; Peel papers.

London. John Murray, publishers.

Oxford. Christ Church Library. Hallam papers.

SECONDARY SOURCES

Barnes, H. E. *A History of Historical Writing*. Norman: University of Oklahoma Press, 1937. A standard history of historiography. Barnes sees Hallam as "more widely read in historical materials than Gibbon or Robertson and rather more faithful to his sources."

Brookfield, Charles, and Brookfield, Frances. *Mrs. Brookfield and Her Circle*. 2 vols. London: Pitman, 1905. The Mrs. Brookfield of the title was a niece of Henry Hallam. This rather disorganized book gives a picture of Hallam in his old age.

Butterfield, H. *The Whig Interpretation of History*. London: Bell, 1931. A critique of the philosophical implications of Whiggism.

————. *The Englishman and His History*. Cambridge: At the University Press, 1944. A defense of the philosophical implications of Whiggism. A better book than the above, it explores the "prehistory" of Whiggism.

Clark, P. "Henry Hallam Reconsidered." *Quarterly Review* 305 (1967): 410–19. A recent article summarizing Hallam's life and work.

Elton, Oliver. *A Survey of English Literature 1780–1830*. 2 vols. London: Arnold, 1912. Elton is one of the warmest champions Hallam has had. Hallam "was much more than erudite; his judgment was ever abreast of his learning." Elton is one of the few people to speak highly of Hallam's style.

Ferguson, Wallace K. *The Renaissance in Historical Thought*. Boston: Houghton Mifflin, 1948. An admirable survey of European and American interpretations of the Renaissance. It places Hallam in context.

Fisher, H. A. L. *Pages from the Past*. Oxford: Clarendon Press, 1939. One essay in this book contrasts Macaulay's warmth and Hallam's cooler conservatism.

Forbes, Duncan. *"Historismus* in England." *Cambridge Journal* 5 (1951): 19–33. Review of historicism and German historical ideas in early nineteenth-century Britain.

————. *The Liberal Anglican Idea of History.* Cambridge: At the University Press, 1952. This book develops the argument of the above article, concentrating on the work of some of Hallam's contemporaries.

Galbraith, V. H. "Good Kings and Bad Kings in English Medieval History." *History* 30 (1945):119–32. A classic article on the historiography of medieval English history.

Gooch, G. P. *History and Historians in the Nineteenth Century.* London: Longmans, 1952. A standard work on the subject, first published in 1913. Hallam receives a few pages. Gooch's method is to concentrate on historians, and something is lost of the general developent of historical ideas and methods. But the range and industry of the work makes it an essential starting point.

Hale, J. R. *England and the Italian Renaissance.* London: Faber and Faber, 1954. Like Ferguson, Hale reviews the literature of the Renaissance. Hale is very good on Hallam's contemporary, Roscoe, and his discussion is much wider than historical literature.

————. *The Evolution of British Historiography.* London: Macmillan, 1967. This is an anthology with a substantial introduction. Hale sees Hallam as "the first great English medieval historian" though "he is not an historian who is willingly read."

Hinton, R. W. K. "History Yesterday." *History Today* 9 (1959): 720–28. Subtitled "Five Points About Whig History," this article reconsiders sympathetically the Whig case.

Jack, Ian. *English Literature 1815–1832.* Oxford: Clarendon Press, 1963. Some appreciative remarks on the *Literature of Europe.* Jack discusses Hallam's work as literature.

Motter, T. H. Vail, ed. *The Writings of Arthur Hallam.* New York: Modern Language Association of America, 1943. An admirable assembly of Hallam's works with a clear framework of his life.

Oliphant, Mrs. *The Literary History of England 1790–1825.* 3 vols. London: Macmillan, 1882. Several perceptive pages on Hallam. Her work, indeed, is unjustly neglected.

Peardon, T. P. *The Transition in English Historical Writing 1760–1830.* New York: Columbia University Press, 1933. A thorough survey of historical writing just before and during Hallam's lifetime. A little unimaginative but valuable for the results of Peardon's industry.

Pocock, J. G. A. *The Ancient Constitution and the Feudal Law.* Cambridge: At the University Press, 1957. Although mainly on seventeenth-century historiography, this book raises questions and problems that relate to all writings on British history. Pocock examines the challenge Brady made to the Cokeian concept of English history.

Raleigh, J. H. "What Scott Meant to the Victorians." *Victorian Studies* 7 (1963):7–34. An important essay, discussing one strand of history and historical consciousness for Hallam's generation.

Ramsden, Guendolen. *Correspondence of Two Brothers.* London: Longmans, 1906. The two brothers are Lord Webb Seymour and the duke of Somerset. There are details of Hallam's friendship with the former. Many letters of Hallam written as a young man.

Smith, R. A. L. "Hallam's History." In *Collected Papers.* London: Longmans, Green, 1947. A short essay, originally published in the *New Statesman* in 1944. Smith praises Hallam's accuracy.

Thompson, James Westfall. *History of History Writing.* 2 vols. New York: Macmillan, 1942. Like Barnes's work, a standard history of historiography. Thompson notes Hallam's fairness.

Weston, C. C. "Henry Hallam." In *Some Modern Historians of Britain,* edited by Herman Ausubel. New York: Dryden, 1951. This article considers Hallam's Whiggism as being a ratification of the present.

Woodward, Sir L. "The Rise of the Professional Historian in England." In *Studies in International History,* edited by K. Bourne and D. C. Watt. London: Longmans, 1967. On the development of history in the generation or two after Hallam. An implicit explanation of why Hallam went out of favor.

Index

Albert, Prince, 22, 32
Allen, Dr. John 16, 42
Amalfi, 13
Anglo-Saxon Studies, 45–46, 96, 112
Anne, Queen, 84, 85
Antwerp, 11
Archaeological Institute, 21–22
Arnold, Dr. Thomas, 22, 32, 33, 43
Athenaeum, 22
Austin, Mrs. Sarah, 31–32

Babbage, Charles, 21
Bacon, Francis, 86, 91, 94–95
Bacon, Roger, 93
Bagehot, Walter, 82, 88
Balmoral, 27
Bancroft, George, 24–25, 27–28
Bayle, Pierre, 106
Belsham, William, 3, 4
Bembo, Pietro, 96
Berington, Joseph, 112
Berne, 11
Birmingham, 1, 5
Bisset, Robert, 62
Blackstone, William, 3, 4, 88, 108
Bolingbroke, Viscount, 111
Boniface VIII, Pope, 41
Bossuet, J.B., 103, 106
Boston, Lincolnshire, 1, 9–10
Boswell, James, 111

Bowood, 13
Brady, Robert, 45, 46, 47, 51–52, 59, 109
British Museum, 22
Britton, John, 113
Brodie, George, 63
Bromley, Kent, 27
Brookfield, Mrs. Jane, 19, 21, 27
Brookfield, Rev. W.H., 19, 21, 29
Brougham, Henry, Lord, 8, 17, 18, 43
Brussels, 11
Buckle, Henry Thomas, 31; *History of Civilisation,* 28
Budapest, 19
Buller, Charles, 116
Burckhart, Jakob, 101
Burghley, Lord, 71
Burke, Edmund, 70, 113
Burnet, Bishop Gilbert, 3, 4, 66, 69, 85, 108, 109, 111
Butler, Charles, 16, 63
Butterfield, Herbert, 58
Byron, Lord, 6

Calais, 11
Calderón, Pedro, 95
Cambridge University, 1, 16, 17, 18, 26, 32, 116
Camden, William, 108–109
Canning, George, 2, 8

Carlisle, Earl of, 23
Carlyle, Thomas, 24, 32, 117
Carte, Thomas, 53–56, 59, 115
Carter, John, 113
Chamonix, 11
Charles I, King of England, 62, 63, 76, 77–81
Charles II, King of England, 82–83, 87, 110
Charles VIII, King of France, 34, 35, 43
Chateaubriand, François, 38
Chaucer, Geoffrey, 97
Chesterfield, Earl of, 111
Chillingworth, William, 106
Cicero, 95, 96, 117
Clevedon, 9, 19, 27, 29
Coates, Thomas, 18
Cobbett, William, 63, 67
Cockburn, Henry, 2
Coke, Sir Edward, 46, 55, 77, 84
Coleridge, Samuel Taylor, 30, 32, 98, 100
Collier, Jeremy, 66–67, 111
Cologne, 11
Constantinople in history, 34, 35
Coxe, William, *House of Austria,* 7, 35
Cranmer, Thomas, 16, 75
Croke, Richard, 92
Cromwell, Oliver, 61, 62, *81–82,* 86
Cromwell, Thomas, 67
Cumberland, Richard, 92

Dalrymple, Sir John, 62, 85, 111
Dante Alighieri, 97
De Lolme, J.L., 2, 56, 61, 88
Descartes, Réné, 94
Dicey, A.V., 61, 88
Dieppe, 5
Disraeli, Benjamin, 90

Donne, John, 98
Dresden, 24
Dryden, John, 7
Dublin, 13

Edinburgh Review, 2, *5–8,* 12, 16, 20, 39, 42, 63–64, 66, 86
Edward the Confessor, King of England, 46, 47
Edward I, King of England, 66
Edward II, King of England, 57
Edward III, King of England, 49, 52, 66, 75
Edward VI, King of England, 64, 68
Eliot, George, 32
Elizabeth I, Queen of England, 57, *69–73,* 74, 75
Elmsley, Peter, 2, 5, 6, 12, 13
Elton, Rev. Sir Abraham, 9
Elton, Charles Abraham, 8, 9, 10
Elton, Oliver, 106
Englefield, Sir Henry, 112
Erasmus, Desiderius, 103, 104, 106
Eton College, 1, 9, 14, 20, 26
Everett, Edward, 23–24, 25

Feudalism, 46–48
Finlay, George, 34
Florence, 13, 26
Fox, Caroline, 33
Fox, Charles James, 62
Fox, Henry, 13
Frederick Barbarossa, German Emperor, 44
Frederick II, Holy Roman Emperor, 40, 42
Freeman, E.A., 34, 45

Galileo Galilei, 91, 94
Garrick, David, 100
Gaskell, James Milnes, 14

Geneva, 11, 12, 13
Gentleman's Magazine, 113
Geological Society, 21
Giannone, Pietro, 42, 109
Gibbon, Edward, 3, 33, 38, 44, 108, 109–10
Gifford, William, 15, 16
Giotto di Bondone, 102
Gladstone, W.E., 2, 19, 20, 26, 27, 117
Gloucester, Duke of (14th century), 53, 54
Godwin, William, 63, 64, 112
Gough, Richard, 109, 113
Gray, Thomas, 6, 90
Great Western Railway, 28
Green, J.R., 45, 49
Gregory VII, Pope, 40, 41, 74
Grotius, Hugo, 84, 91, 92
Guizot, F.P.G., 24, 27

Hallam, Arthur H. (son), 11, 12, 13–14, 17, *18–20,* 21, 26
Hallam, Charles William Waterloo (son), 12
Hallam, Eleanor (mother), 1
Hallam, Eleanor (daughter), 12, 23
Hallam, Henry, birth, 1; school, 1; Oxford University, 2–4, 108–109; lawyer, 4–5; *Edinburgh Review,* 5–8; commissioner of Stamps, 6, 9, 11, 13; travel in Europe, 5, 11–12, 13, 19, 24, 26–27; Royal Society, 13, 95; Society of Antiquaries, 13, 21; London University, 17–18; Society for the Diffusion of Useful Knowledge, 18; Statistical Society, 21; Geological Society, 21; Archaeological Institute, 21–22; British Museum, 22; Athenaeum, 22; Royal Society of Literature, 22

ATTITUDES:
Political reform, 18, 87
Roman Catholicism, 6–7, 38, 39–43, 66, 86, 106
Whiggism, 7, 41, 43, 45, 57–60, *84–87,* 104

WORKS:
Middle Ages, 9, 10–11, 12, 13, 20, 25, *30–60,* 73, 91, 101, 104
Constitutional History, 12–16, 18, 28, 40, *61–87*
Literature of Europe, 20, 28, 31, *89–107,* 117
Supplemental Notes, 25, 31
Literary Essays and Characters, 28
Remains of Arthur Hallam, 14, 19, 20

Hallam, Henry Fitzmaurice (son), 13, 17, 23, 26–27
Hallam, Isaac (great-uncle), 1
Hallam, John (grandfather), 1
Hallam, John, Dean (father), 1, 9
Hallam, Julia (daughter), 27
Hallam, Julia Maria Frances (wife), 9, 11, 12, 13, 23
Hampden, John, 62
Harvard University, 22, 24
Hazlitt, William, 98
Hearne, Thomas, 58, 67
Henry III, King of England, 49
Henry IV, King of England, 50, 52, 55
Henry V, King of England, 50
Henry VI, King of England, 51
Henry VII, King of England, 64
Henry VIII, King of England, 64, 65, 66–67
Henry, Robert, 3, 89, 108, 109
Herbert, George, 98
Herder, J.G., 107
Hobbes, Thomas, 84, 94

Holland House, 8, 12, 13, 15
Holland, Sir Henry, 13, 28, 117
Holland, Lady, *Life of Sydney Smith*, 28
Holland, Lord, 13
Homer, 95, 98
Hooker, Richard, 72, 73, 74, 84, 96, 117
Horner, Francis, 5, 6, 12
Horner, Leonard, 12, 17–18
Hume, David, 3, 4, 36, 38, 45, 46, 47, 48, 52–56, 57, 58–59, 61, 63, 64–66, 67, 69–74, 75, 77, 79, 89, 108, 109, 114
Hunt, Leigh, 15

Inner Temple, 22
Innocent III, Pope, 41
Irving, Washington, 24

Jackson, Dr. Cyril, 2
James II, King of England, 56, 62, 63, 83–85
Jeffrey, Francis, 5–8, 16
Jeffreys, George, Judge, 85
Jerdan, William, 22
Jesse, Midshipman, 19
John, King of England, 49, 66, 74, 75
Johnson, Dr. Samuel, 89, 97, 98, 100, 111–12

Killarney, 13
Kingsley, Charles, 46
Knox, John, 72

Langton, Stephen, Archbishop, 48
Lansdowne, Marquess of, 13, 17, 18, 21
Laud, William, Archbishop, 75–77, 79, 81
Lecky, W.E.H., 104

Leonardo da Vinci, 94
Lewis, M.G., 114
Liddell, Henry, 22
Lincolns Inn, 4
Lingard, John, 20, 40, 42, 66, 112, 115
Lisieux, 27
Livy, 3, 32
Locke, John, 56, 72, 92, 106
Lockhart, John Gibson, 14, 15
London University, 17–18
Long Parliament, 54, 63, 78, 79–80, 82–83
Louis XIV, King of France, 85
Louis XVI, King of France, 62
Lucerne, 11
Luther, Martin, 67, 91, 103, 104, 105
Lyly, John, 98
Lytton, Bulwer, *Harold,* 33, 46

Macaulay, Mrs. Catherine, 62, 64, 115
Macaulay, Thomas Babington, Lord, 16, 20, 23, 25, 27, 28, 32, 50, 63, 75, 80, 85, 86, 95, 117
Machiavelli, Niccolo, 94
Mackintosh, Sir James, 13, 16, 90
Macpherson, James, 62, 85
Magna Carta, 48–49
Mahon, Lord (afterwards Earl Stanhope), 18, 22, 23, 25, 27, 28, 31, 87, 117
Maitland, F.W., 45, 58
Mary I, Queen of England, 64, 97
Melanchthon, Philip, 103, 104, 105
Metaphysical poets, 96, 97–98
Michelangelo, 102
Michelet, Jules, 101
Middle ages, as concept, 34–36, 101
Milan, 12
Millar, John, 48, 61, 62

Milman, Henry Hart, 20
Milner, Joseph, 66, 112
Milnes, Richard Monckton, 23
Milton, John, 3, 63, 80, 85, 100
Mont Cenis, 12
Montesquieu, Charles, 56, 109
Moore, Thomas, 13, 16; *Journal,* 13, 28
More, Sir Thomas, 105
Motley, J.L., 28, 117
Murray, John, 11, 13, *14–16,* 20, 25, 28, 90

Naples, 13
Napoleon, Emperor, 8, 11
Neale, John Mason, 34
Newman, J.H., 32
Nicholas V, Pope, 102
Niebuhr, B.G., 31, 32
Norman Conquest, 46–48
North American Review, 24

Oldfield, Thomas Hinton Burley, 62, 64
Oldmixon, John, 85
Oxford University, 2–5, 17, 22, 32, 43, 116

Petition of Right, 57, 78, 79
Petrarch, F.P., 102
Pinkerton, John, 113
Pope, Alexander, 90
Pugin, A.W.N., 112

Quarterly Review, 8, 14–15, 16, 20, 63

Radcliffe, Mrs. Ann, 114
Raleigh, Sir Walter, 70, 72
Ranke, Leopold von, 31–32
Rapin, Paul de, 3, 56, 108, 109
Raumer, F.L.G., von, 31

Reeve, Clara, 114
Reformation, 39, *66–69,* 76, 97, *103–105*
Renaissance, as concept, 34, 101–102
Revolution of 1688, 18, 41, 48, 50, 51, 53, 55, 59, 60, 63, 77, 80, *83–87,* 110
Richard II, King of England, 50, *52–56,* 59, 66, 74
Ridley, Nicholas, 75
Rienzi, Cola di, 102
Robertson, William, 2, 35, 38, 101, 105, 111, 115
Rogers, Samuel, 23, 95
Rome, 13, 14, 26
Rose, W.S., 13
Royal Society, 13, 95
Royal Society of Literature, 22
Russell, Lord John, 18
Russell, William, 62, 85
Ryde, 24
Rymer, Thomas, 58

Saintsbury, George, 106
Schlegel, August von, 32, 100, 107
Schiller, Friedrich, 32
Scott, Sir Walter, 7, 8, 14, 15, 30, 89, 99, 113, 114
Seymour, Lord Webb, 2, 4, 5, 10, 12
Shakespeare, William, 70, 91, *98–100*
Sheed, William, 29
Sidney, Algernon, 62, 85
Sidney, Sir Philip, 96, 107
Simplon Pass, 12
Sismondi, J.C.L. Simonde de, 13, 90
Smith, Adam, 3, 108, 109
Smith, Sydney, 6, 7, 13
Society for the Diffusion of Useful Knowledge, 18

Society of Antiquaries, 13, 21, 111, 112

Southey, Robert, 3, 8, 14–16, 19, 33, 40, 63, 69, 75, 86

Spa, 11

Spedding, James, 19

Spelman, Sir Henry, 46, 59

Spenser, Edmund, 96, 97

Stanley, A.P., 32

Statistical Society, 21

Stewart, Dugald, 92, 94

Strafford, Earl of, 16, 76, 79, 81

Stuart, Gilbert, 112

Stubbs, William, 45, 49, 56, 58, 116

Suffolk, Earl of (14th century), 53

Tasso, Torquato, 3

Taylor, Jeremy, 106

Tennyson, Alfred, 18, 19–20, 21, 26, 46, 95; *In Memoriam,* 19, 26

Tennyson, Emily, 18–19

Tennyson, Septimus, 123n.86

Thackeray, W.M., 19, 21, 27

Thirlwall, Connop, 32

Ticknor, George, 24, 117

Trench, Richard Chenevix, 19

Tupper, Martin, 95

Turin, 12

Turner, Sharon, 112

Venice, 12, 24, 26; its history, 35

Vergil, 3

Victoria, Queen of England, 27, 32

Vienna, 19

Voltaire, F.M.A. de, 38, 44, 109

Walpole, Horace, 62, 107, 113, 114

Warton, Thomas, 89

Waterloo, 11

Webster, Daniel, 24

West Bromwich, 1, 4, 9

Whateley, Richard, 114

Whishaw, John, 15, 16, 17

Wiesbaden, 24

William I, King of England, 46, 47

William III, King of England, 85

Windsor, 1, 4

Wintour, Anna, 13, 19

Wintour, Harry, 2, 13

Wordsworth, William, 75, 95, 100

Wyatt, James, 113

Wycliffe, John, 67

Yelverton, Christopher, 72, 74

Zwingli, Huldreich, 103